#3

Annamalai Swami
Final talks

Edited by David Godman

Other titles written or edited by David Godman

Be As You Are
No Mind - I am the Self
Papaji Interviews
Living by the Words of Bhagavan
Nothing Ever Happened (three volumes)
The Power of the Presence (three volumes)
Sri Ramana Darsanam
Padamalai
Ramana Puranam

Information on these titles can be found at www.davidgodman.org

© David Godman 2006

Reprint March 2018

ISBN 0-9711371-6-1

Published by
David Godman
Avadhuta Foundation
P. O. Box 296
Boulder, CO 80306-0296
USA

Printed at
Sudarsan Graphics
27, Neelakanta Mehta St,
T. Nagar, Chennai - 17
India

BHAGAVAN SRI RAMANA MAHARSHI

Sri Annamalai Swami

Introduction

Annamalai Swami came to Bhagavan in 1928 and spent nearly all of the following ten years serving him, initially as his attendant, and subsequently as the supervisor of all the building projects that Sri Ramanasramam undertook during this period. The full story of Annamalai Swami's association with Bhagavan has already been told in his autobiography, *Living By The Words of Bhagavan*. Many of the stories that Annamalai Swami alludes to in this book are recorded fully, in their proper context, in this earlier work.

In 1938 Bhagavan instructed Annamalai Swami to stop working in Sri Ramanasramam, saying that in future he should devote himself to solitary meditation in Palakottu, the community of *sadhus* that grew up on the western border of Sri Ramanasramam. Bhagavan even went so far as to say that Annamalai Swami should not visit him in the ashram any more. However, the harshness of this edict was considerably softened by the fact that Bhagavan came to Palakottu every day and often visited Annamalai Swami in his home, a small house that Bhagavan himself had helped to design. After Bhagavan passed away in 1950, Annamalai Swami lived and did *sadhana* in this house for many years, devoting all his energies to carrying out the spiritual teachings that Bhagavan had imparted to him. Annamalai has said that his years of constant meditation in the 1950s and 60s finally brought him to a continuous awareness of the Self.

In the 1980s devotees, many of them foreigners, began to visit Annamalai Swami in order to get instructions on Bhagavan's teachings. Some of the dialogues from this period appeared as the final portion of *Living By The Words of Bhagavan*. The visitors to his ashram and the readers who subsequently encountered these teachings in his book were often surprised by the elegant and trenchant way in which Annamalai Swami passed on the teachings that had been given to him by his Master. Though he had had virtually no formal education, his deep experience of the subject matter enabled him to communicate it with rare authority.

Unfortunately, very few of these sessions were recorded, so there is little record of these teaching sessions that took place in the 1980s and 90s. However, in 1995, the year that Annamalai Swami finally passed away at the age of eighty-nine, audio recording were made of the sessions that took place between March and October. This small book is an edited record of what turned out to be the last six months of Annamalai Swami's teaching career.

Annamalai Swami's teachings were uncompromising, straightforward, and rarely deviated from a solid core of advice that he himself had been given by his own Guru. However, they were delivered with a force and a gentle humour that was irresistibly attractive. In the last few years of his life his small room was invariably packed on the afternoons that he dispensed his wisdom. In offering this book to the general public, it is my hope that it will be found to be as useful and stimulating as the earlier collection of teachings.

May the blessings of Bhagavan be on this small but valuable teaching record.

David Godman, Tiruvannamalai, October 1999

1

Annamalai Swami: Mind is just a shadow. Attempts to catch it and control it are futile. They are just shadows chasing shadows. You can't control or eliminate a shadow by chasing it or by putting a shadow hand on it. These are just children's games.

Ram Tirtha once told a story about a small boy who ran down the street, trying to catch up with the head of his shadow. He never managed because no matter how fast he ran, the shadow of his head was always a few feet ahead of him.

His mother, who was watching him and laughing, called out, 'Put your hand on your head!'

When the boy followed this instruction, the shadow hand caught up with the shadow head. This was enough to satisfy the boy.

This kind of advice may be enough to keep children happy, but it won't produce satisfactory results in the realm of *sadhana* and meditation. Don't chase your shadow thoughts and your shadow mind with mind-control techniques because these techniques are also shadows. Instead, go back to the source of the shadow-mind and stay there. When you abide in that place, you will be happy, and the desire to go chasing after shadow thoughts will no longer be there.

Bhagavan often told the story of a man who tried to get rid of his shadow by burying it in a pit. This man dug a hole and then stood on the edge of it in such a way that his shadow was cast on the bottom of the hole he had just made. After lining it up in this way, he started throwing soil on the shadow in an attempt to bury it. Of course, no matter how much soil he put in the hole, the shadow still remained on top of it.

Your mind is an insubstantial shadow that will follow you around wherever you go. Attempts to eliminate or control it cannot succeed while there is still a belief that the mind is real, and that it is something that can be controlled by physical or mental activity.

Question: But this shadow mind must still be eliminated by some means.

Annamalai Swami: When Self-realisation happens, mind is no longer there. However, you do not get Self-realisation by getting rid of the mind. It happens when you understand and know that the mind never existed. It is the recognition of what is real and true, and the abandonment of mistaken ideas about the reality and substantiality of this ephemeral shadow you call the mind.

This is why Bhagavan and many other teachers kept bringing up the analogy of the snake and the rope. If you mistake a rope on the ground for a snake, the snake only exists as an idea in your mind. That idea might cause you a lot of worry and anxiety, and you may waste a lot of mental energy wondering how to avoid the snake or kill it, but this fact remains: there is no snake outside your imagination. When you see the rope, the substratum upon which your false idea of a snake is superimposed, the idea that there is a snake, and that it is real, instantly vanishes. It is not a real snake that has disappeared. The only thing that has disappeared is an erroneous idea.

The substratum upon which the false idea of the mind has been superimposed is the Self. When you see the mind, the Self, the underlying substratum, is not seen. It is hidden by a false but persistent idea. And conversely, when the Self is seen, there is no mind.

Question: But how to give up this false idea that the mind is real?

Annamalai Swami: The same way that you give up any wrong idea. You simply stop believing in it. If this does not happen spontaneously when you hear the truth from a teacher, keep telling yourself, 'I am not the mind; I am not the mind. There is no mind; there is no mind. Consciousness alone exists.' If you have a firm conviction that this is the truth, one day this firm conviction will mature to the point where it becomes your direct experience.

Consciousness alone exists. If you generate a firm conviction that this is the truth, eventually this firm conviction will become your own direct experience.

Consciousness alone exists. That is to say, whatever exists is consciousness alone. Keep this in mind and don't allow yourself to regard anything else as being real. If you fail and give even a little reality to the mind, it will become your own false reality. Once this initial wrong identification – 'I am the mind, the mind is real' – has happened, problems and suffering will follow.

Don't be afraid of the mind. It's a false tiger, not a real one. Something that is not real cannot harm you. Fear and anxiety may come to you if you believe that there is a real tiger in your vicinity. Someone may be making tiger noises as a joke to make you afraid, but when he reveals himself, all your fears go because you suddenly understand that there never was a tiger outside your imagination.

Question: One can have a temporary experience of the Self, the underlying reality, but then it goes away. Can you offer any guidance on how to stabilise in that state?

Annamalai Swami: A lamp that is lit may blow out if the wind is strong. If you want to see it again, you have to relight it. But Self is not like this. It is not a flame that can be blown out by the passing winds of thoughts and desires. It is always bright, always shining, always there. If you are not aware of it, it means that you have put a curtain or a veil in front of it that blocks your view. Self does not hide itself behind a curtain. You are the one who puts the curtain there by believing in ideas that are not true. If the curtain parts and then closes again, it means that you are still believing in wrong ideas. If you have eradicated them completely, they will not reappear. While these ideas are covering up the Self, you still need to do constant *sadhana*.

So, going back to your question, the Self does not need to stabilise itself. It is full and complete in itself. The mind can be stabilised or destabilised, but not the Self.

Question: By constant *sadhana*, do you mean self-enquiry?

Annamalai Swami: Yes. By strength of practice, by doing this *sadhana*, this veil will be removed completely. There will be no further hindrances. You can go to the top of Arunachala, but if you are not alert, if you are not paying attention, you may slip and end up at Easanya Math [a Hindu institution at the base of the hill].

You have to make an enormous effort to realise the Self. It is very easy to stop on the way and fall back into ignorance. At any moment you can fall back. You have to make a strong determined effort to remain on the peak when you first reach it, but eventually a time will come when you are fully established in the Self. When that happens, you cannot fall. You have reached your destination and no further efforts are required. Until that moment comes, constant *sadhana* is required.

Question: Is it important to have a Guru at this stage, this period when constant effort is required?

Annamalai Swami: Yes. The Guru guides you and tells you that what you have done is not enough. If you are filling a bucket with water, you can always add more if there is still space. But when it is completely full, full to overflowing, it is pointless to add even a single drop. You may think that you have done enough, and you may believe that your bucket is full, but the Guru is in a better position to see that there is still a space, and that more water needs to be added. Don't rely on your own judgement in this matter. The state you have reached may seem to be complete and final, but if the Guru says, 'You need more *sadhana*,' trust him and carry on with your efforts.

Bhagavan often used to say, 'The physical Guru is outside, telling you what to do and pushing you into the Self. The inner Guru, the Self within, simultaneously pulls you towards itself.'

Once you have become established in the inner Guru, the Self, the distinction between Guru and disciple disappears. In that state you no longer need the help of any Guru. You are That, the Self.

Until the river reaches the ocean it is obliged to keep on flowing, but when it arrives at the ocean, it becomes ocean and the flow stops. The water of the river originally came from the ocean. As it flows, it is merely making its way back to its source. When you meditate or do *sadhana*, you are flowing back to the source from which you came. After you have reached that source, you discover that everything that exists – world, Guru, mind – is one. No differences or distinctions arise there.

Non-duality is *jnana*; duality is *samsara*. If you can give up duality, *Brahman* alone remains, and you know yourself to be that *Brahman*, but to make this discovery continuous meditation is required. Don't allocate periods of time for this. Don't regard it as something that you do when you sit with your eyes closed. This meditation has to be continuous. Do it while you are eating, walking, and even talking. It has to be continued all the time.

2

Question: How does the *jnani* relate to his body? How does it feel to him?

Annamalai Swami: The *jnani* is not really aware of the body. Or if he is, he feels it like *akasha*, space itself.

After one of the operations to remove the tumour on Bhagavan's arm had been completed, I was worried enough to send a girl who worked for me to the ashram to ask how Bhagavan was. I could not go myself because Bhagavan had asked me not to visit him.

When this girl told Bhagavan why she had come, he started laughing very loudly. I interpreted this to mean that nothing had really happened. His laughter was a message to me that Bhagavan was not his body and that I should therefore not be upset or worried by anything that happened to it.

Years before, I was walking on the hill with Bhagavan when he remarked, 'I don't feel the weight of the body at all. I feel as if I am walking weightlessly through the sky.'

I sometimes have the same feeling when I am walking around.

Question: I was not here yesterday, but it seems that someone asked a question about the vibration that comes off a *jnani*. You also apparently talked about the vibrations that ordinary people and bad people give off. Can you repeat what you said?

Annamalai Swami: A *jnani's* vibrations stay even after he leaves the body. All people leave vibrations in the places they have been and lived. *Jnanis* leave a good vibration and bad people leave a bad vibration. I am not talking about a gross physical phenomenon that everyone can feel. The vibration that a *jnani* leaves is subtle. Radio broadcasts can only be heard if one has a radio that is tuned to the right frequency. You tune into a *jnani's* vibrations by having a quiet, still mind. This is the 'wavelength' of the broadcast. If you have not tuned yourself to receive this frequency, you cannot expect to experience or benefit from the vibrations that a *jnani* may have left in a place.

Question: Is the intensity of the vibration more if we stay close to a living *jnani*?

Annamalai Swami: Yes.

Question: Is it the same with Arunachala?

Annamalai Swami: Yes. No doubt about it. Bhagavan himself has said that if one lives at the foot of Arunachala, one does not need any kind of initiation. If one's intentions are pure and holy, merely living here can be a good *sadhana*. Guhai Namasivaya, a saint who lived on the hill a few centuries ago, said in one of his poems that this Arunachala hill draws seekers in the same way that a magnet attracts iron. In ancient times the *shakti*, the power of this hill was hidden, but Bhagavan made it open to everybody.

Bhagavan sang about this in *Aksharamanamalai*, verse 98: 'I have made public your doings. Do not hate me for this.'

It was rare for Bhagavan to make such an open declaration about something that he had done or accomplished. He rarely used the word 'I' when he referred to some event that had happened in earlier eras of his life. Sometimes he would use the passive form: 'something happened to me....' At other times he would go to the extreme of using someone else's name when he was telling a story about something that had happened to himself.

Question: I am going back to Europe for two months. It may be longer because there is a possibility that I may have to prolong the trip.

Annamalai Swami: Even if you prolong your trip, Arunachala will pull you back. Pulling back is its nature in the same way that a magnet's nature attracts iron. Once you establish a connection with Arunachala, it will keep on pulling you towards it. You cannot resist.

Question: So is it dangerous for us to come and visit this place?

Annamalai Swami: It is only dangerous for the ego. Until we become one with Arunachala, it will pull us to kill our ego. The water in a river cannot rest where it is. The force of gravity compels the water to flow downwards, back to its original source.

Question: You said that merely living near Arunachala could be good *sadhana*. The same thing must be true of living near a *jnani*. You have told many stories about how living with Bhagavan transformed people, even those who were not making much effort to meditate or do any other formal *sadhana*.

Annamalai Swami: Yes, we were all immeasurably benefited by being in his presence, by doing ordinary, everyday things with him. He was always available to give advice about *sadhana* if anyone wanted to ask about it, but we were also benefited by his presence and by the example he set on how to live life properly.

For much of the time Bhagavan would appear to be a lenient, tolerant, easy-going father. If we didn't follow his instructions about various aspects of our lives, it would seem for a while that he was allowing us to go our own way. Sometimes it would even seem as if he was were approving some of the wrong things that we were doing, but slowly, when the time was right, he would lead us back to his own way.

Question: So when people did things that were really bad, he didn't complain or interfere?

Annamalai Swami: When Bhagavan lived in Mango Tree Cave, a man called Jada Swami gave him a lot of trouble. At the beginning of their relationship, whenever Jada Swami conducted a *puja*, he would invite Bhagavan along and then ask him to bang the drum at the culmination of the ceremony. This effectively relegated Bhagavan to being a minor functionary in Jada Swami's *puja*. Jada Swami would put on quite a good show, so much so that many passing pilgrims or members of the public would be attracted to these ceremonies. It helped, of course, that Jada Swami cut a very imposing figure. With his long matted hair and fierce look, he looked like an archetypal ascetic *sadhu*.

However, many people attending the *pujas* noticed the radiant expression on the face of the young boy who was banging the drum, and some of them began to prostrate to him because they could detect something of his radiant holiness.

Jada Swami got very jealous when he saw this happening, but he tried to recoup some of his self-esteem by telling these visitors, 'He is my disciple, so you can do *namaskar* to him as well'.

Bhagavan never objected when Jada Swami behaved like this or made untrue claims about his being a disciple.

When it became clear that Bhagavan was going to attract a big following of his own, Jada Swami got jealous and tried to drive him off the hill. On one occasion, when Bhagavan was sitting outside Virupaksha Cave, Jada Swami even tried to kill him by rolling a big boulder onto him. Bhagavan, who was sitting with his back to Jada Swami, got an early warning of the attack when he heard some little pebbles cascading down the rock behind him. Bhagavan jumped up and caught Jada Swami red handed.

When he confronted him and asked him what he was doing, Jada Swami tried to bluff his way out of it by saying that he was just playing a practical joke.

'I was just doing it to see if you would get afraid,' he said.

Bhagavan never criticised him, even after this incident, and the two of them continued to live side by side on the hill for several years afterwards.

Question: This behaviour, these things that Jada Swami did, they are not the sort of thing that one would expect from a *sadhu* living on Arunachala.

Annamalai Swami: Guhai Namasivaya, who lived on the hill several centuries ago, was also well known for his bad temper. In one famous incident, he cursed a group of weavers who had been causing him trouble. Within a short time, all their businesses failed. The curse was apparently a long-lasting one, for in the years that followed, all attempts to start weaving businesses in Tiruvannamalai failed.

Question: So would you say that Bhagavan was very tolerant of people who treated him badly?

Annamalai Swami: Yes. He never responded in a negative way to criticism. Sometimes he would even laugh when people said bad things about him. He was indifferent to praise and blame. They didn't touch him.

When Perumal Swami printed his insulting book about Bhagavan, Bhagavan simply said, 'Keep the book in front of the ashram so that people can read it there. The good people won't believe it, but when the bad people read it, they will stay away and leave me in peace.'

This happened in the 1930s at a time when large crowds of people were starting to come to Ramanasramam. Perumal Swami did a good job of distributing the book himself, for many of the casual visitors from town stopped coming. It was a bit of a break for us because many people would just come at meal times, hoping to get a free meal. These freeloaders were a disturbance for all of us.

Sundaram [Annamalai Swami's translator]: The same thing is happening here. We cooked a special meal for Punarvasu and invited some devotees to eat. Without telling Swami, one man brought seventeen extra people, none of whom were devotees. We had never seen any of them before. We had only cooked food for fifteen people. If one or two extra people had come, we could have managed, but we couldn't give a meal to all these extra people. We divided the food up into very small quantities and fed all these unknown people who had just shown up to eat. When the meal was over, they started wandering around, making a nuisance of themselves. They disturbed the people who were still cooking in the kitchen and they stole the sandals of one of our devotees.

Swami doesn't mind meeting with *sadhaks* who want to discuss important spiritual matters, but he doesn't like these functions where lots of people come. He is very weak most of the time, and he wants to save his energy for important matters.

Annamalai Swami: [laughing] I just give *vibhuti* to most of the people who come. But no matter how much I discourage visitors, they still come, often for no good reason at all. I am physically weak, so I can only deal with people for short periods nowadays. I am a bit like a well that is fed by a small spring. A few people taking buckets of water out at the same time will empty the well. Then they will have to wait some time for the water to flow in again before they can take more water.

3

[A devotee who came to Annamalai Swami had so much pain in one of his legs, he found it very difficult to sit comfortably on the floor. After Annamalai Swami had observed the difficulties the man was having, he made the following remarks:]

Annamalai Swami: Though the body is needed for *sadhana*, one should not identify with it. We should make good use of it, and look after it well, but we should not pay too much attention to it.

There are so many thoughts in the mind. Thought after thought after thought; they never stop. But there is one thought that is continuous, though it is mostly subconscious: 'I am the body.' This is the string on which all other thoughts are threaded. Once we identify ourselves with the body by thinking this thought, *maya* follows. It also follows that if we cease to identify ourselves with the body, *maya* will not affect us any more.

Maya is fundamentally non-existent. Bhagavan said that *maya* literally means 'that which is not'. It is unreal because everything that *maya* produces is an outgrowth of a wrong idea. It is a consequence of taking something to be true that is not really true. How can something that is not real produce something that is real? If a barren woman says that she has been beaten by her son, or that she has been injured by the horns of a hare, we would rightly take her to be deluded. Something that does not exist cannot be the cause of suffering or of anything else.

Maya may appear to be real, to have a real existence, but this is a false appearance. The truth is: it is not real; it has no existence at all.

How to get rid of this 'I am the body' feeling and of the *maya* that is produced by it? It goes when there is *saman bhava*, the equanimity or equality of outlook that leaves one unaffected by extreme opposites such as happiness and unhappiness, pleasure and pain. When *saman bhava* is attained, the idea 'I am the body' is no longer present, and *maya* is transcended.

Question: Is the body to be regarded as unreal, as 'not me'? What attitude should I have towards this body and all the sensory information it provides me with?

Annamalai Swami: By itself, this body is *jada*, inert and lifeless.

Without the mind, the body cannot function. And how does the mind function? Through the five senses that the body provides.

Mind and body are like the tongue and teeth in the mouth. They have to work in harmony with each other. The teeth do not fight with the tongue and bite it. Mind and body should combine in the same harmonious way.

However, if we want to go beyond the body, beyond the mind, we have to understand and fully accept that all the information the senses provide is not real. Like the mirage that produces an illusory oasis in the desert, the senses create the impression that there is a real world in front of us that is being perceived by the mind. The apparent reality of the world is an illusion. It is merely a misperception. When the mind perceives a snake where in reality there is only a rope, this is clearly a case of the senses projecting an imaginary image onto a real substratum. This, on a large scale, is how the unreal appearance of the world is projected by the mind and the senses onto the underlying reality of the Self.

Once this happens, we see the superimposition, the unreal names and forms we have created, and we forget about the substratum, the reality that underlies them. Many examples are given by our teachers and by our spiritual books. If you see a carved wooden elephant, for example, at some point you forget that it is only wood. You see the form of the carving, and your mind gives that form the name 'elephant'. While your mind is registering this name and this form, you are no longer registering the object as a block of wood. It is the same when you see jewellery made out of gold. You see a shape, call it a ring or a necklace, and while you are studying the form, you temporarily forget the substance it is made of.

Self-enquiry is the process by which attention is put on the substratum instead of on the names and forms that are habitually imposed on it. Self is the substratum out of which all things appear to manifest, and the *jnani* is the one who is continually aware of the real substratum. He is never deluded into believing that the names and forms that are perceived by the senses have any real existence.

Whatever we see in this room, for example that picture of Bhagavan over there, is unreal. It has no more reality than the objects we perceive in our dreams. We think we live in a real, materially substantial world, and that our minds and bodies are real entities that move around in it. When the Self is seen and known, all these ideas fade away and one is left with the knowledge: Self alone exists.

Question: If I regard all the people that I see and meet as unreal projections, what do I base my moral sense on? I can go around killing them or robbing them without feeling guilty because I would know that they are just characters in my dream.

Annamalai Swami: Everything that we perceive is *maya*, an unreal dream, but one should not then think, 'Since everything is unreal, I can do what I like'. There are dream consequences for the bad acts committed in the dream, and while you still take the dream to be the reality, you will suffer the consequences of your bad behaviour. Do no evil and have no hate. Have equanimity towards everything.

[Annamalai Swami then turned to a devotee who had been sitting motionless, with his eyes closed, in front of him.]

If you sit in meditation for a long time, without moving the body, the mind gets dull and tamasic. Even moving the toes while sitting is a good way of getting rid of the *tamas*. Mirabai used to dance and sing. That's a good way to meditate. *Giri pradakshina* [walking around Arunachala] is also good. It's walking meditation.

4

Annamalai Swami: Today I am going to tell you a story I once heard. A rich man lived in a village. From his youth till his old age he had spent all his time accumulating wealth. He owned many houses and vast tracts of land. As his material wealth increased, his ego expanded with it. He enjoyed boasting about his wealth.

One day, as he was sitting in front of his house with a stick in his hand, a poor man who was known to be a little stupid passed by.

'Why are you holding that stick in your hand?' he asked.

The rich man decided to have some fun with him.

'It's a special stick,' he replied. 'It has to be given to an idiot. This stick is passed from person to person, and each person who receives it must pass it on to someone who is more stupid than he is.'

Giving him the stick, he continued, 'Now it is your turn to own it. You must keep it with you until you find someone who is an even bigger idiot than you.'

The poor man humbly accepted the stick and began his quest to find someone whom he felt had even less intelligence than he did. Since he was, by a long way, the least intelligent person in the village, he could not find anyone to give the stick to.

A few weeks later he heard that the rich man was sick and dying. He went to visit him, partly to pay his last respects, and partly to tell him that he hadn't managed to find anyone to give the stick to. He took his custody of the stick very seriously and he wanted advice from the rich man on what he should do with it.

After some preliminary conversation about the rich man's health and the fate of the stick, the poor man asked the rich man what was going to happen to all his money when he died.

'I have to leave all my money here,' answered the rich man. 'I don't know where and when I shall be reborn, but I do know that I can't take any of my money with me. I shall have to start off with nothing again.'

He relapsed into a glum silence, not relishing the prospect of being parted from his money.

The poor man, who had never really considered this aspect of dying before, thought about it for a while and then came to a conclusion.

'You must have the stick,' he said, handing it back to him, 'because I have suddenly realised that you are an even bigger idiot than I am. Though you have had a long life and many opportunities, you have accumulated nothing of value that you can carry forward with you. You have no peace of mind because you are worried about losing your money, and you have accumulated no good karma because you have spent your whole life pursuing selfish ends. In a few days the piles of money you have amassed will have the same value for you as piles of garbage. This money will have no value for you in your next life. By devoting your entire life to the accumulation of things that will ultimately prove to be of no use, you have demonstrated that you are a worthy recipient of the stick.'

He placed the stick on the rich man's bed and left.

That reminds me of a strange comment a disciple once made about his Guru. He called his Guru a 'heap of garbage' and referred to himself as a hen.

When he was asked about this, he replied, 'A hen can always find something good to eat so long as it keeps busy scratching around in the garbage. But effort is required. If the hen stops scratching, the supply of food stops.'

Question: I wasn't here yesterday, but I was told that someone asked the following question: 'I have been following Bhagavan's teachings for many years, but without any obvious benefits. I don't feel any peace. What am I doing wrong? Why am I not getting results?'

Annamalai Swami: Self-enquiry must be done continuously. It doesn't work if you regard it as a part-time activity. You may be doing something that doesn't hold your interest or attention, so you think, 'I will do some self-enquiry instead'. This is never going to work. You may go two steps forward when you practise, but you go five steps backward when you stop your practice and go back to your worldly affairs. You must have a lifelong commitment to establish yourself in the Self. Your determination to succeed must be strong and firm, and it should manifest as continuous, not part-time, effort.

For many lifetimes you have been immersed in ignorance. You are habituated to it. All your deeply rooted beliefs, all your patterns of behaviour reinforce ignorance and strengthen the hold it has over you. This ignorance is so strong, so deeply enmeshed in all your psychological structures, it takes a massive effort over a long period of time to break free from it. The habits and beliefs that sustain it have to be challenged again and again.

Ignorance is ignorance of the Self, and to remove it Self-awareness is required. When you come to an awareness of the Self, ignorance vanishes. If you don't lose contact with the Self, ignorance can never arise.

If there is darkness, you remove it by bringing light. Darkness is not something real and substantial that you have to dig out and throw away. It is just an absence of light, nothing more. When light is let into a dark room, the darkness is suddenly no longer there. It did not vanish gradually or go away piece by piece; it simply ceased to exist when the room became filled with light.

This is just an analogy because the Self is not like other lights. It is not an object that you either see or don't see. It is there all the time, shining as your own reality. If you refuse to acknowledge its existence, if you refuse to believe that it is there, you put yourself in an imaginary darkness. It is not a real darkness. It is just your own wilful refusal to acknowledge that you are light itself. This self-inflicted ignorance is the darkness that has to be banished by the light of Self-awareness. We have repeatedly to turn to the light of the Self within until we become one with it.

Bhagavan spoke about turning inwards to face the Self. That is all that is needed. If we look outwards, we become entangled with objects and we lose awareness of the Self shining within us. But when, by repeated practice, we gain the strength to keep our focus on the Self within, we become one with it and the darkness of Self-ignorance vanishes. Then, even though we continue to live in this false and unreal body, we abide in an ocean of bliss that never fades or diminishes.

This is not going to happen in a moment because lifetimes of wrong and ignorant thinking have made it impossible for most of us to focus intently and regularly on the Self within. If you leave your house and start walking away from it, and if you continue this habit over many lives, you will probably be a long, long way from home when you finally decide that you have had enough and that you want to go back to the place from where you started. Don't be discouraged by the length of the journey, and don't slacken in your efforts to get home. Turn 180° to face the source of your outward journey, and keep moving back to where you started. Ignore the pain, the discomfort, and the frustration of seeming not to get anywhere. Keep moving back to your source, and don't let anything distract you on the way. Be like the river on its journey back to the sea. It doesn't stop, take diversions, or decide to flow uphill for a while. It doesn't become distracted. It just moves slowly and steadily back to the place from where its water originated. And when the river dissolves in the ocean, river is no more. Only ocean remains.

Jiva [the individual self] came from Siva and has to go back to Siva again. If there is a big charcoal fire, and one burning ember jumps out, the fire in the ember will soon go out. To reignite it, you have to put it back into the fire, back into its burning source.

There is no happiness in separation. The *jiva* has no happiness, contentment or peace so long as it remains a separate being. The separate being comes from the Self. It has to go back there and end there. Only then will there be eternal peace.

The energy of the mind comes from the Self. In the waking state the mind functions as a separate entity. In the sleep state it goes back to the source. Again and again it comes out and goes back. It does this because it doesn't know the truth of what it really is. It is Self and Self alone, but its ignorance of this fact makes it miserable. It is this feeling of separateness that gives rise to desires, suffering and unhappiness. Keep the mind in the Self. If you can do this, you can live in peace both while you are awake and also while you are asleep. In deep sleep all differences are dropped. If you keep the mind in the Self during the waking state, there will also be no differences, no distinctions. You will see everything as your own Self.

5

Question: How can we recognise a *jnani*?

Annamalai Swami: For a mature seeker there is one principal symptom of being in the presence of a *jnani*. If the seeker's mind becomes quiet, without any effort, then this is a good indication. But this is not a test that is valid or conclusive for everyone. If an immature seeker sits in the presence of a *jnani*, his or her mind will probably remain just as active as ever. It is very difficult for ordinary people to determine who is and who is not a *jnani*. There are no consistently reliable tests.

This reminds me of a story that was told by Ramakrishna. A *sadhu* was sitting in *samadhi* in the shade of a tree by the side of the road.

A man who was walking down the road glanced at the *sadhu* and thought, 'He's probably drunk'. The *sadhu* was shaking a little and the passerby assumed it was a drunken tremble.

Another man walked by, but his train of thought led him to a different conclusion: 'This man looks happy. He is probably waiting for his girlfriend to come.'

The sun was setting as the next man came along. He saw this shadowy figure sitting under the tree and thought, 'He may be a thief. He is probably hiding under that tree so that he can jump out and attack people who pass by. I will give him a wide berth just in case he turns out to be dangerous.'

He took a little detour through the fields because that made him feel safer.

Shortly afterwards a fourth man came along. He was an advanced spiritual seeker and in the gathering gloom he could detect a halo of light around the *sadhu's* head.

'This must be an enlightened man,' he thought, and so he went up to him and prostrated.

People perceive *jnanis* through the distorting prisms of their minds. More than that they cannot do. If you put on yellow glasses, everything you see will be coloured yellow. Change the colour of the lenses, and the colour of what you perceive also changes. The *jnani* has no distorting lenses or prisms to obscure, fragment or change his vision. He sees everything as God, as his own Self.

Question: How do we get this unobscured, unfragmented vision?

22

Annamalai Swami: Bhagavan wrote in *Ulladu Narpadu* that perceived objects are of the same nature as the one who perceives them. In the waking state the gross physical eyes see gross physical objects. In the dream state the subtle eye sees subtle dream-world objects. Beyond that there is the eye of the Self. Since the Self is infinite and immaterial, what it 'sees' is infinite and immaterial. The *jnani*, being Self alone, sees and knows only the Self.

[Annamalai Swami was referring to verse four: 'If one is a form, the world and God will also be so. If one is not a form, who can see their forms and how? Can what is seen be of a different nature to the eye? Self, the eye, is the limitless eye.'
Bhagavan's explanation of this verse can be found in Maha Yoga *(1973 ed. p.72):*

'If the eye that sees be the eye of flesh, then gross forms are seen; if the eye be assisted by lenses, then even invisible things are seen to have form; if the mind be that eye, then subtle forms are seen; thus the seeing eye and the objects seen are of the same nature; that is, if the eye be itself a form, it sees nothing but forms. But neither the physical eye nor the mind has any power of vision of its own. The real Eye is the Self; as He is formless, being the pure and infinite Consciousness, the Reality, He does not see forms.'

Annamalai Swami now continues with his answer:]

The Self shines all the time. If you can't see it because your mind has obscured it or fragmented it, you have to control your vision. You have to stop observing with the eye of the mind, because that eye can only see what the mind projects in front of it. If you want to see with the eye of the Self, switch the projector of the mind off. The infinite eye of the Self will then reveal to you that all is one and indivisible.

Question: Going back to the question of how to determine who is and who is not a *jnani*, can we not come to some valid conclusion by studying his life and his teachings? Will not his state be somehow reflected in the life he leads?

Annamalai Swami: You cannot determine the answer to this question by studying the teachings or the behaviour of a person you think might be a *jnani*. These are not reliable indicators. Some *jnanis* may stay silent; others may talk a lot. Some are active in the world; some withdraw from it. Some end up as teachers while others are content to stay hidden. Some behave like saints, whereas others act like madmen. The same peace can be found in the presence of all these beings, since this peace is not affected by modes of behaviour, but there may be no other common factors.

Question: *Jnanis* are supposed to have an equality of vision. Can we not decide whether someone may be a *jnani* on the basis of whether he treats people around him equally?

Annamalai Swami: *Jnanis* remain absorbed in the Self at all times and their apparent behaviour is just a reflection of the circumstances they find themselves in. Some may appear to be egalitarian. Others may not. They play their allotted roles, and though they may seem to be involved in them as ordinary people would be, they are not really touched by any of the events that occur in their lives. Equal vision may be there, internal equanimity may be there, but don't expect all *jnanis* to behave in a prescribed, egalitarian way.

Bhagavan often used to cite King Janaka as an example of a *jnani* who was fully involved in the affairs of the world. But when his palace caught fire and was burning to the ground, he was the only person in the vicinity who was not disturbed.

In this same story there was a group of *sadhus* who lived near the palace. When the fire began to spread, they panicked and began to collect their sticks, their spare *kaupinas*, their water pots, and so on. They had very few possessions, but they were still very attached to them, and they definitely didn't want to lose them to the fire. They were more worried about their spare underwear than Janaka was about his palace. Janaka watched his palace burn to the ground with complete equanimity. When you have this *jnana*, your inner peace is a solid rock that cannot be disturbed.

Being rich and being a king will not obstruct *jnana*. It's just a question of having the right attitude. There is a story in *Yoga Vasishta* about a king called Mahabali. He had lost interest in his kingdom, his riches and his pleasures because he had developed a strong desire for *jnana*. He summoned his Guru, Sukacharya, to the court and asked him what he should do to attain *jnana*. Mahabali was assuming that Sukacharya would tell him to renounce his kingdom and go to the forest and meditate.

Instead Sukacharya told him, 'I am the Self. You are the Self. All is the Self. That's all you need to know to attain this *jnana* you are looking for. I cannot give you any lengthy teachings today because I have to go and attend a meeting of the gods. Anyway, lengthy teachings are not needed. Just remember the words I have told you. If you can hold on to this knowledge "I am the Self" at all times, no further practice or initiation will be necessary.'

There is another story about Janaka that I like. A man called Sukabrahman called on Janaka for spiritual advice.

'I am a seeker of truth,' he said. 'What can you tell me?'

'What did you see while you were coming here?' asked Janaka.

'I saw houses made of sugar,' answered Sukabrahman. 'I saw streets made of sugar. I saw trees and flowers made of sugar. I saw animals made of sugar. I saw your palace and saw that it was made of sugar. Everything I saw was made of sugar. As I stand here, I see that you are made of sugar and that I also am made of sugar.'

Janaka laughed and said, 'You are a ripe soul. You don't need any teaching. You are already a *jnani*.'

Question: Some people realise the Self just by hearing the Guru's words. How is this possible?

Annamalai Swami: Disciples who are spiritually very advanced can realise the Self as soon as they hear the truth from an enlightened Guru, because the words of such a being have great power. If you are in this advanced state, they will reach your inner core and reveal to you the peace that is your real nature. When the Guru tells you that you are the Self, there is a power and an authority in those words that can make them become your own reality. If you are pure and ready, no practice will be required. One word from a *jnani* and his state will become yours too.

Question: How does the mind project this world I see in front of me?

Annamalai Swami: Everything we see in this waking state is a dream. These dreams are our thoughts made manifest. Bad thoughts make bad dreams and good thoughts make good dreams, and if you have no thoughts, you don't dream at all. But even if you do dream, you must understand that your dream is also the Self. You don't have to suppress thoughts or be absolutely thoughtless to abide as the Self. If you know that even your waking and sleeping dreams are the Self, then the thoughts and the dreams they produce can go on. They will not be a problem for you any more. Just be the Self at all times. In this state you will know that everything that appears to you is just a dream.

Question: What I am trying to say is, 'How do thoughts and desires create this world we live in?' It doesn't seem possible that all this that I see could be a manifestation of my hidden desires.

Annamalai Swami: Imagine that a man has to catch a train at 3 a.m. He goes to bed thinking, 'I have to wake up before that so I can catch this train'.

Then, sometime during the night he has a dream in which he wakes up at 2.30. He remembers the train journey, gets out of bed, goes to the station, boards the train, and takes his seat.

Then he thinks, 'I got up early this morning. I am a bit sleepy. I will lie down and have a nap.'

He stretches himself out and goes to sleep.

The next morning he wakes up at 8 a.m. in his own bed at home and realises that he has missed his train. His whole journey had just been a dream that had been provoked by the thought, 'I must wake up before 3 a.m.'.

The waking state, which you take to be real, is just an unfolding dream that has appeared to you and manifested in front of you on account of some hidden desire or fear. Your *vasanas* sprout and expand miraculously, creating a whole waking-dream world for you. See it as a dream. Recognise that it is just an expansion of your thoughts. Don't lose sight of the Self, the substratum on which this vast, believable dream is projected. If you hold onto the knowledge 'I am the Self', you will know that the dreams are also the Self, and you won't get entangled in them.

Question: 'All is one' may be the truth, but one can't treat everything in the world equally. In daily life one still has to discriminate and make distinctions.

Annamalai Swami: I once went for a walk near the housing board buildings [government flats that were built in the 1970s about 300 metres from Annamalai Swami's ashram]. There was a sewage trench on one side of the building. I could smell the stench of the sewage even though I was a long way away. I stayed away from it because I didn't want to be nauseated by the bad smell.

In circumstances such as these you don't say, 'All is one. Everything is the Self,' and paddle through the sewage. The knowledge 'everything is the Self' may be there, but that doesn't mean that you have to put yourself in dangerous or health-threatening places.

When you have become one with the Self, a great power takes you over and runs your life for you. It looks after your body; it puts you in the right place at the right time; it makes you say the right things to the people you meet. This power takes you over so completely, you no longer have any ability to decide or discriminate. The ego that thinks, 'I must do this,' or, 'I should not do that,' is no longer there. The Self simply animates you and makes you do all the things that need to be done.

If you are not in this state, then use your discrimination wisely. You can choose to sit in a flower garden and enjoy the scent of the blooms, or you can go down to that trench I told you about and make yourself sick by inhaling the fumes there.

So, while you still have an ego, and the power of discrimination that goes with it, use it to inhale the fragrance that you find in the presence of an enlightened being. If you spend time in the proximity of a jnani, his peace will sink into you to such an extent that you will find yourself in a state of peace. If, instead, you choose to spend all your time with people whose minds are always full of bad thoughts, their mental energy and vibrations will start to seep into you.

I tell you regularly, 'You are the Self. Everything is the Self.' If this is not your experience, pretending that 'all is one' may get you into trouble. Advaita may be the ultimate experience, but it is not something that a mind that still sees distinctions can practise.

Electricity is a useful form of energy, but it is also potentially harmful. Use it wisely. Don't put your finger in the socket, thinking, 'All is one.' You need a body that is in good working order in order to realise the Self. Realising the Self is the only useful and worthy activity in this life, so keep the body in good repair till that goal is achieved. Afterwards, the Self will take care of everything and you won't have to worry about anything any more. In fact, you won't be able to because the mind that previously did the worrying, the choosing and the discriminating will no longer be there. In that state you won't need it and you won't miss it.

Question: What should be the right attitude when one sits in the presence of a *jnani*?

Annamalai Swami: Just keep quiet. Make contact with the silence of the Self within. This is the way of making contact with your Guru, and it is also the best attitude to have when you are sitting in his presence.

Question: I understand. This is also my inner feeling, my own belief of what I need to do. But knowing it does not produce the desired results. I know that I can make contact with my real Guru by abiding as the Self within, but it rarely happens. I cannot abide in that state all the time. And when I am out of that state, I am acutely aware of the separation. Then, when I feel that separation, I feel a need to be in the Guru's physical presence. The advice, 'Go back to the Self within' is not so attractive then, because I know I can't do it.

Annamalai Swami: Who is feeling the separation? Who is separate from whom? Ask yourself this question whenever these thoughts arise.

I remember a devotee who got very attached to Bhagavan's feet. He would touch his feet and then try to hold on to them for a long time.

One day Bhagavan said to him: 'Don't get attached to the feet because one day they will disappear. If you are so attached to physical things, when they go, you will be depressed and you will feel miserable. Hold onto the Self within. That is the Guru's true feet. It will never go away because it is eternal. The Self abides within you as your Guru. It is up to you to find him there and to stay with him.'

The light of the Self cannot be extinguished. It is eternal and immanent. It is not like ordinary lights that can be switched on and off. Once it is discovered within, it will be on all the time.

[The incident that Annamalai Swami reported in his final answer also seems to have been recorded by Sadhu Natanananda in his Tamil book, Sri Ramana Darshanam. *In a section about devotees who wanted to hold onto the Guru's feet or show excessive respect to him, he has Bhagavan give out two emphatic statements: the first to a devotee who was holding onto his feet, and the second to another devotee who was performing an over-elaborate prostration:*

'Only the Supreme Self, which is ever shining in your Heart as the reality, is the Sadguru. The pure awareness, which is shining as the

inward illumination "I", is His gracious feet. The contact with these [inner holy feet] alone can give you true redemption. Joining the eye of *reflected consciousness [chidabhasa], which is your sense of individuality, to these holy feet, which are the real consciousness, is the union of the feet and the head which is the real significance of the word* asi *[the verb in* tat tvam asi, "that thou art"]. As these inner holy feet can be held naturally and unceasingly, hereafter, with an inward-turned mind, cling to that inner awareness which is your own real nature. This alone is the proper way for the removal of bondage and the attainment of the supreme truth.'*

'The benefit of performing namaskaram [prostrating] to the Guru is only the removal of the ego. That is not attained except by total surrender. Within the Heart of each devotee the gracious Guru is giving darshan in the form of consciousness. Since to surrender is to offer fully, in silence, the subsided ego, which is a name-and-form thought, to the aham sphurana [the effulgence of "I"], the real holy feet of the gracious Guru. Since this is so, Self-realisation cannot be attained by a bowing of the body, but only by a bowing of the ego.']

6

[A foreign woman came to see Annamalai Swami. While she was prostrating to him she seemed to become unconscious of her surroundings and she remained lying on the floor at his feet for about ten minutes. This was not the first time that she had fallen into this state while in Annamalai Swami's presence. After watching her for some time, he shouted at her:]

Annamalai Swami: You should not go into *laya* [a trance-like state] like this! It is becoming a habit with you. It may give you some kind of temporary happiness, but it is not a happiness that helps you spiritually. It is the same as sleep. Even worldly activities are better than this *laya*. Get out of this habit!

[Addressing the other people present] People occasionally went into states like this in front of Bhagavan. He never encouraged them, even the ones who appeared to be in a deep meditation.

I remember one occasion when Bhagavan noticed a man who had been sitting motionless in the hall for at least an hour, apparently in a deep meditation. Bhagavan was not fooled.

He called to Kunju Swami and others who were present, 'Shout at him, shake him, and when he wakes up, take him on *giri pradakshina*! This is no better than sleep. This state is not good for him. He is just wasting his time sitting like this.'

Bhagavan warned us about this state, and he often cited stories of *sadhus* who had been stuck in this state for years. One of the most frequently told was a story about a *sadhu* who asked his disciple for a glass of water. While he was waiting for the man to return, he went into a deep *laya* state that persisted for many, many years. He was in this state so long, his disciple died, the river changed its course, and different rulers came and went.

When he opened his eyes, his first comment was, 'Where is my glass of water?' Before he went into *laya*, this thought was uppermost in his mind, and decades later, this thought was still there.

Bhagavan's comment on this story was, 'These states are not helpful. They are not *samadhi*.'

[The woman who had been in laya *then asked the next question:]*

Question: Whenever I start meditating, soon after I start, I fall into these states. How can I prevent these *laya* states from coming and taking me over?

Annamalai Swami: Keep practising self-enquiry. This is the way to avoid *laya*. The mind usually has two habits; either it is occupied with many thoughts and engaged in activities, or it goes back to sleep. But for some people, there is this third option, falling into this *laya* state. You should not indulge in it because once it becomes a habit, it becomes addictive. It is a pleasant state to be in, but if you fall very deeply into it, it becomes very hard to get out of it.

You know what this state is like because you have been in it many times. As soon as you feel the first symptoms of an approaching trance, get up and walk around. Don't remain sitting or lying. Walk around or do some work, and above all, keep up the practice of self-enquiry. If you practise self-enquiry constantly, you will never find yourself falling into *laya*.

You can conquer this habit. You just need to be attentive and to do self-enquiry.

7

Question: Bhagavan once remarked, 'What is the value of knowing God if we don't know the name of our own "I"?' He also spoke about the 'I-I' vibration, saying that it was an emanation of the Self. When Bhagavan spoke of 'I-I', did he mean that it was *shabd nadi*, a subtle sound, or is it merely the feeling 'I-I'?

Annamalai Swami: They both indicate and mean the Self.

Question: Is the sound also the Self?

Annamalai Swami: The sound is happening in the Self.

Question: Is it the same as the Self, or is it the reflection?

Annamalai Swami: It is also a part of the Self.

Question: So is it like the white colour of milk – inseparable from the milk?

Annamalai Swami: Yes.

Question: I am asking this because I hear the sound all the time, but I don't know if I feel the 'I-I' in the Heart. There is a feeling that I ought to be going deeper, so I ask myself, 'What is the feeling of the sound?' Is this a good practice?

Annamalai Swami: Let me give you an example. The fan over our heads is spinning around. A stream of cool air is coming from it but we also hear the noise of the motor. Both perceptions originate from the working of the fan. It is the same with the Self. The soundless sound of the Self goes on all the time by itself. It doesn't make a sound; it *is* the subtle sound. If you tune into this sound – you can't actually listen because it is not a physical noise – that tuning in will lead you to the peace of the Self. That peace is prior to and beyond this very subtle pulsation. When you reach that final peace, that ultimate stillness, the sound will disappear in the Self. In that final place there is no sound, there is only peace, somewhat like the peaceful soundless state that is experienced in deep sleep. However, full awareness remains there. It is not an unconscious state.

Most people cannot hear or be aware of the subtle inner vibration because it is drowned out by the physical noise of the outer world and by the persistent mental noise of the mind. The only people who can hear this sound are those in whom thoughts have mostly disappeared. One needs to be in a deep level of mental peace in order to be aware of this sound.

This subtle vibration is resonating all the time in all people, but virtually no one hears it because preoccupation with thoughts covers it up. Bhagavan was not the first teacher to talk about this subtle sound. Himaleka, for example, mentioned it in *Tripura Rahasya*, so this inner sound is not something newly discovered. Close your mental and physical ears and you will hear this vibration resonating all the time.

Question: As I mentioned before, I hear the sound all the time, but I feel that the experience is not deep enough to take me back to an absorption in the Self. I say this because I am not experiencing the peace that Swami is talking about, the peace in which the sound disappears and leaves peace alone. I am trying to go deeper. I am asking myself where the feeling of the sound comes from because I want to remain in the Heart, in bliss.

Annamalai Swami: Enquire 'Who am I?' or 'What is my real nature?' The nature of the Self is nothing but peace. If you are not aware of that peace, it means that you are identifying with something that is not the Self. As long as you hear, taste and smell things, you identify with the body. When the perceptions and the perceiver of them vanish, you become aware of the peace that is there all the time.

Question: I hear the sound. Then I ask myself who is hearing the sound, and the answer is 'I'. What happens next depends on where I am. If I am in Swami's presence or in the meditation hall at Sri Ramanasramam, I feel the presence of the Self and the bliss of peace, but when I am away from Swami, it is not so easy.

Annamalai Swami: You need not hold on to That because you *are* That all the time. That is enough. You *are* That. How can you hold on to That, or feel separate from it, or try to get it back, or lose it? If That is your real nature, how can you pretend that you are nearer to it in two places and separate from it when you are somewhere else?

Question: I have the experience of That with Swami, but I don't have that same experience when I am away from him. This is definitely my experience, so I don't really understand what you are telling me.

Annamalai Swami: Your understanding or your lack of it does not affect the truth of what I am saying. You are That. See who you are and there will be nothing obstructing the experience of this fact.

Question: I still say I see who I am when I am near Swami. When I am away from him, I can remember it as a fact, but it is not my direct experience.

Annamalai Swami: This is because you identify with your body and your mind. Your mind is making you believe that a certain experience can only happen when you are in a particular place. Give up this identification and you will find that the Self is everywhere. You will see it, know it and be it wherever you go. Everything is Swami, including you yourself.

Question: How do I give up identification with the body, particularly when I am not in front of Swami? I keep practising, but I don't have that experience.

Annamalai Swami: Meditate 'I am the Self'. If you do this, the idea that you are the body will go. 'I am the Self' is still an idea, and as such, it belongs in *maya*, along with all other ideas. But you can begin to conquer *maya* by giving up utterly wrong ideas that bind you and cause you trouble. How to do this? Replace them with ideas that are a better reflection of the truth, and which are helpful in leading you to that truth. If you want to cut iron, you use another piece of iron.

In battle, if someone shoots an arrow at you, you shoot one back. In *maya*, if the arrow of a bad idea comes speeding towards you, dodge it. Don't let it stick to you or you will end up in pain. Then, in retaliation, fire back the arrow of 'I am the Self' at the place where the wrong idea came from.

Sadhana is a battlefield. You have to be vigilant. Don't take delivery of wrong beliefs and don't identify with the incoming thoughts that will give you pain and suffering. But if these things start to happen to you, fight back by affirming, 'I am the Self; I am the Self; I am the Self'. These affirmations will lessen the power of the 'I am the body' arrows and eventually they will armour-plate you so successfully, the 'I am the body' thoughts that come your way will no longer have the power to touch you, affect you or make you suffer.

This fight all takes place within *maya* because in reality you are peace and peace alone. But while you are suffering in *maya* you can use these thoughts as a means of ultimately conquering it.

Question: To remain as myself, to have this awareness 'I am the Self,' is it enough that I merely hear this sound, 'I-I', because I do hear it everywhere?

Annamalai Swami: If it is constant, it will be enough. If you don't forget your real Self, that will be enough. Your real Self is everything. Not an atom exists apart from the Self. You, the real you, the Self, are all inclusive. When I say give up your identification with the 'I am the body' idea, I don't mean that you are not the body. I mean that you should give up the idea that you are only the body. You are all bodies, all things, all creation, but paradoxically, this knowledge will not come to you unless you give up identifying with particular objects, such as 'I am the body' and limiting thoughts such as 'I am so-and-so'. When you have given up all thoughts, all identifications, the true knowledge suddenly dawns on you: 'I am the unmanifest Self and I am also the whole of manifestation.'

So I tell people: 'This physical body is not you; the mind is not you. Go beyond them to see what is really behind them.' This is done to make people give up their incorrect, limiting ideas, so they can have a direct experience of what is truly real. I am asking people to be aware of the rope of reality instead of being confounded and led astray by the mental illusion of the snake.

Question: This 'I'-thought seems to vibrate at the same speed as the sound and the feeling of 'I-I'. So when I think 'I', it reminds me of the sound. This seems to happen by itself. But afterwards, I need to think 'I' to remind me of this vibration that is going on.

Annamalai Swami: Since you forget your real Self, the only way is to go back to your real Self. If you keep the light on all the time, darkness cannot enter your room. Even if you open the door and invite it to come in, it cannot enter. Darkness is just an absence of light. In the same way, mind is just a self-inflicted area of darkness in which the light of the Self has been deliberately shut out. You live in the darkness by insisting on believing ideas that have no validity, and you live in the light of the Self when you have given up all ideas, both good and bad.

Question: So you are saying that believing that I am a body and a particular person is purely imagination. Or better still, a bad habit that I should try to get rid of?

Annamalai Swami: Correct. This habit has become very strong because you have reinforced and strengthened it over many lifetimes. This will go if you meditate on your real Self. The habit will melt away, like ice becoming water.

Question: Bhagavan once remarked that free will is non-existent, that all our activities are predetermined and that our only real choice is either to identify with the body that is performing the actions or with the underlying Self in which the body appears.

Someone once said to him: 'If I drop this fan, will that be an act that has always been destined to happen in this moment?'

And Bhagavan replied, 'It will be a predestined act'.

I assume that these predestined acts are all ordained by God, and that as a consequence, nothing happens that is not God's will, because we, as individuals, have no power to deviate from God's ordained script.

A question arises out of this. If I remember the Self, is this God's will? And if I forget to remember at a certain moment, is this also God's will?

Or, taking my own case, if I make an effort to listen to the sound 'I-I', is this God's will, or is it individual effort?

Annamalai Swami: Forgetfulness of the Self happens because of non-enquiry. So I say, 'Remove the forgetfulness through enquiry'. Forgetfulness or non-forgetfulness is not a part of your destiny. It is something you can choose from moment to moment. That is what Bhagavan said. He said that you have the freedom either to identify with the body and its activities, and in doing so forget the Self, or you can identify with the Self and have the understanding that the body is performing its predestined activities, animated and sustained by the power of the Self.

If you have an oil lamp and you forget to put oil in it, the light goes out. It was your forgetfulness and your lack of vigilance that caused the light to go out. Your thoughts were elsewhere. They were not on tending the lamp.

In every moment you only have one real choice: to be aware of the Self or to identify with the body and the mind. If you choose the latter course, don't blame God or God's will, or predestination. God did not make you forget the Self. You yourself are making that choice every second of your life.

Question: In Swami's book someone asked him, 'I am making decisions, but I don't feel that I am making these decisions. It is just my destiny or divine will.'

You answered him by saying that this was correct, but now you are saying that whether or not one does self-enquiry is nothing to do with destiny at all.

Annamalai Swami: The Self is always present. Nothing obstructs your awareness of it except your self-inflicted ignorance. Our efforts, our *sadhana*, are directed towards removing this ignorance. If this ignorance is removed, the real Self is revealed. This revelation is not part of destiny. Only the outer bodily activities are destined.

Question: So my inner life is my own responsibility. I cannot blame Bhagavan if I am not remembering myself.

Annamalai Swami: Bhagavan is always present, inside you and in front of you. If you don't cover the vision of Bhagavan with your ego, that will be enough. The ego is the 'I am the body' idea. Remove this idea and you shine as the Self. That is the only thing you need to do in this life. The various events of your life – all the things that are going to happen to you – they are all destined. If you don't want them to happen, they will still occur, even if you try to avoid them. And if you want things that are not in your destiny, they won't come to you.

There is no point worrying about the outer events of your life because you can exercise no control over these destined activities. Your responsibility in this life is to see who you are, not to rewrite your life script.

Question: I can therefore blame God, destiny or Bhagavan for everything that happens to me in this world. But at the same time I have to assume responsibility for everything that goes on inside me.

Annamalai Swami: Correct. This Bhagavan you speak of is not a body, a person who existed at some time. All is Bhagavan; all is Ramana. There can be no mistakes in following Bhagavan's path because Bhagavan is like an eternal light that is always burning, a grace that is always giving. To be aware of Bhagavan is to be aware of this inner truth. If you are not aware of this Bhagavan, it is your responsibility, not his. He is not hiding from you; you are hiding from him. He does not think that he is separate from you. It is you who believe that you are separate from him.

Question: The outside world is a miserable, confusing place. There is not much going on there that helps us to remember who we really are.

Annamalai Swami: Yes, you can say that this state of affairs is also Bhagavan's grace, Bhagavan's compassion. You could say that he keeps the world like this as an incentive to go inwards. This state of affairs sets up a real choice: if we go outwards there are problems; if we go inwards there is peace.

Question: I want to ask about some other aspect of this that sometimes troubles me. The desire to become absorbed in the Self seems to be some kind of *vasana*. It is still a desire, and to indulge in it implies that I must look for something that I don't already have. With this attitude I then feel that I am setting up enlightenment as some kind of future goal, and not as something that is here and now. There is something very dualistic in this attitude, and I sometimes get the feeling that I am not accepting Bhagavan's will for the present moment if I am looking for something that is not here and now.

Annamalai Swami: This desire is not counterproductive. The desire for enlightenment is necessary because without it you will never take the necessary steps to realise the Self. A desire to walk to a particular place is necessary before you take any steps. If that desire is not present, you will never take the first step. When you realise the Self, that desire will go.

Question: Though I know that the Self is changeless, it seems to me that my experience of it is different in different moments. Sometimes it is more intense, deeper. The peace and the bliss are felt more intensely at certain times. The mind wants more peace, more bliss. It is not content with merely hearing or feeling the *aham sphurana* [the 'I-I' emanation]. Is this creating a problem for me? Is my desire to keep going with my *sadhana* correct?

In each moment I am having some experience of something that doesn't change: I am either hearing or feeling the *aham sphurana*. But always there is this desire to go deeper, to be feeling more peace, more bliss. I am not satisfied with the experience I am having. Is this desire to do more *sadhana* a good desire, or is it interfering with Self-awareness?

Annamalai Swami: Your ultimate need is to get established in the changeless peace of the Self. For this you have to give up all thoughts. If this has happened to you, nothing more is needed. If you are in the real state, there will be no wants, no desire to push on to some other state. In realisation there will be no desire for anything else, and no doubt about whether anything is needed. This final state is just peace. There are no desires and doubts there.

Question: I am not experiencing the peace that Swami is talking about. I must therefore need to do something more.

Annamalai Swami: See who you are. That is the only advice I can give you. You are peace. Be that peace and there will be no hankering for anything else.

Question: The problem seems to be asking for that peace, desiring it.

Annamalai Swami: The one who is asking is not you. The thoughts that come and go are not you. Whatever comes and goes is not you. Your reality is peace. If you don't forget that, that will be enough.

8

[The subject of this conversation is a verse that Bhagavan wrote in 1913. It originally appeared in Sri Ramana Gita, *and was later incorporated into* Ulladu Narpadu Anubandham, *the* Supplement to Forty Verses.*

'In the interior of the Heart-cave Brahman *alone shines in the form of the Self with direct immediacy as "I", as "I". Enter into the Heart with questing mind or by diving deep or through control of breath, and abide in the Self.']*

Question: In *Ulladu Narpadu Anubandham* Bhagavan mentions the three paths: self-enquiry, observation of breathing, and diving within the heart. Could you please say something about this diving? What it is, how it happens?

Annamalai Swami: The result of following these three paths is the same: Self-realisation. And it can also be said that the three paths are also the same, although at first sight the description of them makes it sound as if three totally different techniques are being described.

Bhagavan said, 'Do self-enquiry. Find out who you really are. When you are totally absorbed in this problem, this enquiry will lead you to the Self.' Some people, though, said that they found this very hard, or they said that this method somehow didn't appeal to them. Bhagavan would sometimes tell such people to watch the breath, to see where it arose. Bhagavan always maintained that mind and breath arose in the same place, so focusing attention on the source of the breath is really the same as focusing attention on the source of the mind through self-enquiry. The third option is diving within. This is not a separate path. It is just another description of what happens when you follow self-enquiry, or when you find the source of the breath through intense observation. 'Diving within' means putting your whole mind on the Self. When the one-pointed intensity to discover the Self is there, diving in happens and the mind goes back to its source and merges there.

Question: So there is no special method for diving within. It happens by itself. Is this true?

Annamalai Swami: It doesn't happen by itself. You have to go on making an effort until the point where you become totally effortless. Up till that moment your effort is needed. The mind only gets dissolved in the Self by constant practice. At that moment the 'I am the body' idea disappears, just as darkness disappears when the sun rises.

Question: I have read several books about the practical side of Bhagavan's teachings. Mouni Sadhu wrote about the 'I'-current. Osborne wrote about a current that is not physical, but which can be felt physically. My understanding is that these writers were describing a current of some sort that helps *sadhaks* to be aware. It is said in these books that it can be felt very strongly. What is this current? Is it a special grace of Ramana, or is it common to all paths?

Annamalai Swami: Ramana and other Gurus only show us the way. We have to walk on the path ourselves to realise the truth. If you want to go to America, having someone tell you where it is and how to get there will not magically transport you to that place. You have to go to the airport and get on the plane yourself. You have to carry out the instructions the Guru has given you until you realise the truth for yourself. Grace takes us to the Guru. Grace shows us the way home by guiding us in the right direction, but we still have to do the work ourselves.

Question: My question is not so much about grace itself. It is about this 'I'-current that I have been reading about. Is it the grace of Ramana? Is it the grace of the Self? I don't know the answer to this question, but I feel this current very strongly inside me.

Annamalai Swami: This current, this 'I am' consciousness, is present within all of us. It is not something special that devotees of one particular Guru have. It is our nature, and as such it is common to all. But only a few souls are mature enough or ripe enough to be aware of it. Though it is present within all of us, grace puts us in touch with it and gives us a taste of what it is like. And once that taste is there, the thirst to realise the Self follows.

Tayumanuvar, a Tamil saint whom Bhagavan often quoted, wrote in one of his poems:

'My Guru merely told me that I am consciousness. Having heard this, I held onto consciousness. What he told me was just one sentence, but I cannot describe the bliss I attained from holding onto that one simple sentence. Through that one sentence I attained a peace and a happiness that can never be explained in words.'

Question: When Bhagavan spoke about the death experience that happened to him when he was about sixteen years old, he said, 'I held my breath and kept my lips tightly closed so that no sound could escape. Neither the word "I" nor any other word could escape.' Why did he do this?

Annamalai Swami: He did not want mental energy to escape through the mouth. The five senses are always moving outwards in an attempt to engage the world. The mouth is one of the channels through which the five senses move outwards into the world. When the mind and the breath are restrained, when mental energy is not moving outwards to engage with the world and its objects, the mind starts to go back to its source. At sixteen Bhagavan may not have known this, but this is effectively what happened.

This death experience was something that happened to him. It did not occur as a result of something that he consciously did.

Question: Bhagavan wanted to know the answer to the question 'Who am I?' He seemed to find the answer straight away. When I ask the question, when I try to find out what the Self is, I can reject thoughts that arise as being 'not me', but nothing else happens. I don't get the answer that Bhagavan did, so I am beginning to wonder why I am asking the question.

Annamalai Swami: You say that you are not getting the right answer. Who is this 'you'? Who is not getting the right answer?

Question: Why should I ask? Asking has not produced the right answer so far.

Annamalai Swami: You should persist and not give up so easily. When you intensely enquire 'Who am I?' the intensity of your enquiry takes you to the real Self. It is not that you are asking the wrong question. You seem to be lacking intensity in your enquiry. You need a one-pointed determination to complete this enquiry properly. Your real Self is not the body or the mind. You will not reach the Self while thoughts are dwelling on anything that is connected with the body or the mind.

Question: So it is the intensity of the enquiry that determines whether I succeed or not.

Annamalai Swami: Yes. If enquiry into the Self is not taking place, thoughts will be on the body and the mind. And while those thoughts are habitually there, there will be an underlying identification: 'I am the body; I am the mind.' This identification is something that happened at a particular point in time. It is not something that has always been there. And what comes in time also goes eventually, for nothing that exists in time is permanent. The Self, on the other hand, has always been there. It existed before the ideas about the body and the mind arose, and it will be there when they finally vanish. The Self always remains as it is: as peace, without birth, without death. Through the intensity of your enquiry you can claim that state as your own.

Enquire into the nature of the mind by asking, with one-pointed determination, 'Who am I?' Mind is illusory and non-existent, just as the snake that appears on the rope is illusory and non-existent. Dispel the illusion of the mind by intense enquiry and merge in the peace of the Self. That is what you are, and that is what you always have been.

9

Question: Has Swamiji realised the Self?

Annamalai Swami: Yes. But this is sometimes a strange question to answer. It is like having somebody ask you if you have become a human being. You are always a human being. You didn't have to do anything to accomplish it. You are self-evidently a human being, so much so, it is strange to field questions about it.

Question: It is not self-evident to me.

Annamalai Swami: Then find out who you are.

Question: How does one find out who one is?

Annamalai Swami: You will find out by constantly doing self-enquiry. Ask yourself, 'Am I the body? Am I the mind?' When self-enquiry is deepened, you understand who you are.

Question: How long did it take for Swamiji to find out?

Annamalai Swami: If one is mature, one can realise it in this moment. If one is not mature one has to take up *sadhana* to make oneself receptive to the truth.

Question: Which category were you in?

Annamalai Swami: I served Bhagavan for more than twelve years. After that I came to this place because I wanted to be more established in the Self. After several years of *sadhana* I realised the Self.

Question: Is Swamiji totally established in the Self?

Annamalai Swami: Yes.

Question: What happens in your deep sleep state? Is it the same as when you are awake?

Annamalai Swami: Yes.

Question: I have heard that when people came close to Ramana Maharshi, they could feel a penetrating peace. As I sit here in the presence of Swamiji I feel nothing. Why is this?

Annamalai Swami: Not everyone felt peace in Bhagavan's presence. Madhava Swami served Bhagavan as his personal attendant for many years, but he claimed he felt no peace there. He used to have the same complaint as you.

In his later days he would say, 'People are saying that whenever they are in the presence of Bhagavan they feel tremendous peace. But when I go inside Bhagavan's hall, it is like hell for me.'

I am telling you this because the answer to your question is, 'Whether you feel peace or not in a *jnani's* presence depends on your maturity'. People who are mature are sensitive to the *jnani's* presence. Such people will immediately experience peace when they come into the presence of a *jnani*. Others have to wait. Buds that are ready to bloom open when the sun's rays fall on them. Those who are not ready have to wait.

Question: In other words, is it because of my immaturity that I am not able to feel peace in the presence of Swamiji?

Annamalai Swami: Don't make this kind of judgement about yourself. Don't think that you are not mature. If you hold onto this kind of thought, this will be a hindrance to your realisation, because the truth is already within you.

Question: But Swamiji just said that if a person were mature, he would be able to feel peace in the presence of a realised soul.

Annamalai Swami: Maturity and immaturity belong to the mind. You are not the mind; you are already the Self.

Question: Are there differences in the degree of realisation of the Self? For example, Ramana was widely acclaimed as a *Sadguru*. Is your understanding the same as Ramana's?

Annamalai Swami: You see a big lamp before you. Your own lamp is unlit. So you bring your lamp to the lamp which is already burning. And when you go away from that lamp, you have your own lamp, your own light. Wherever you go, from that point on, the light is with you. The state of *jnana* is the same for all. Anyone who realises the Self is in the same state of peace, which is beyond the mind.

Though the experience of the Self is the same in all cases, it is true that some *jnanis* end up helping a lot of people, whereas others, who are equally enlightened, may help fewer people. Some *jnanis* do not teach at all. They live ordinary lives and are rarely, if ever, recognised for what they really are.

Water can be in a well or it can be in a lake. It is the same water, but one source can quench more thirsts than the other. A small lamp can light up a room, whereas a big one can light up a whole street. Bhagavan was one of those big, blazing lights that could light up a huge area. He guided and brought light to many people.

Question: Swamiji is saying that some *jnanis* are big lamps and that others are small. Do the small lamps become bigger, or do they always remain the same?

Annamalai Swami: Whichever light you go to, the light is always the same. This business of the lamps is just an example. What I am trying to say is, only a few people have the capacity to guide a large number of people towards the truth. Realising the truth is one thing, but guiding others towards it is something else. All *jnanis* are not equally capable when it comes to guiding others.

Question: But my question was, 'Do the little lamps become big lamps, or are they always destined to be little?'

[A devotee of Annamalai Swami, who was clearly irritated by this line of questioning, then interrupted and asked, 'Why are you repeating the question? Have you just come here to test Swamiji's state?']

Annamalai Swami: This kind of questioning will not help you to realise the Self. Questions such as these will disappear if you have a strong desire for realisation. Your mind will then not be occupied with such thoughts. You can ask me many questions and I can give you any number of answers. We could go on like this for hours, but neither your questions nor my answers would give you any kind of contentment. Having such questions in your mind will not lead you to an experience of the Self.

I would advise you to question yourself, 'Who is asking the question? And who is getting the answer?' If you have this attitude towards your doubts and your questions, your quest for their source will lead you back to the Self. In that place there are no questions and no answers. There is only peace.

Question: I want to ask one last question. What is the significance of Arunachala? Last night was full moon. So many people went round the hill. I also went.

Annamalai Swami: It is not an ordinary hill. It is not like other hills in the world. It is a spiritual hill. Those who associate with it feel a magnetic pull towards the Self. Though it is in the form of a hill, it has the full energy of the Self. Seekers who come to this place with the intention of realising the Self can be much benefited by going round the hill. Walking round the hill can help you a lot with your *sadhana*.

There is water everywhere under the ground, but there are some places where it is easier to get at. Likewise, the Self is everywhere. There is no place that is without it, but it is also true that there are certain places, certain people, around which and around whom the presence of the Self can be easily felt. In the proximity of this hill, the presence of the Self is more powerful and more self-evident than anywhere else. However, the great glory of this hill cannot be explained in words. One has to experience it for oneself.

We often say, 'I slept happily,' but if someone asks you to explain in words the happiness you felt in that state, what can you say? You can experience it, but you can't really explain it.

This is how the Self is. You can experience it, you can become it, but you cannot explain this state through words. The same thing can be said about this hill. You can experience it, but you can't explain it in a satisfactory way.

In Indian mythology we have a wish-fulfilling tree. If you find this tree and tell it what you want, your wish will be granted. Arunachala also has this reputation. That is why so many people come here on a full moon night and walk around it. But very few people come here and ask for enlightenment, for undisturbed peace. All beings are ultimately searching for undisturbed peace, but who asks for it here? If you are ready to receive peace, Arunachala can give it to you.

This peace is already within us, but people don't appreciate this, so they go looking for it all over the place, in external locations.

Question: Is it faith in Arunachala that produces results, or is there some inherent power here that is independent of my belief in it?

Annamalai Swami: You can say that Arunachala is a light. It shines whether you believe in it or not. If you go near a lamp, it will shine on you whether you believe in it or not. Arunachala is the light of the Self, and the light of the Self will continue to shine, even if you refuse to believe that it is there.

Question: Is Arunachala the only place that is like this, or are there other places? I have heard that there are powerful places in the Himalayas.

Annamalai Swami: Bhagavan himself said that Arunachala is greater than all other religious places. There are other holy, powerful places in the world, but none has the power of Arunachala. Bhagavan has written about this in his verses.

There is a huge amount of *shakti*, spiritual energy, here. We can take as much as we want, but no matter how much we take, the original amount is never diminished. It is an inexhaustible source. Even before Bhagavan came and lived here, there were innumerable sages who had discovered the power of Arunachala for themselves. Many came here, realised the Self and attributed their realisation to the power and grace of this mountain. Bhagavan has praised this mountain in his poetry, and other sages have talked about the spiritual greatness of Arunachala in their verses and in their other teachings.

Though others have praised the mountain, they did not succeed as well as Bhagavan in making Arunachala and its power famous all over the world. Bhagavan has revealed the secret of Arunachala, which is why so many foreigners now come here.

Bhagavan always maintained that the power of this mountain was not a matter of belief. He said that if you sit in the shade of a tree, you will feel the cool shade. This is a physical fact, not a matter of belief. Then he went on to say that Arunachala worked in the same way. It affects the people who are here, whether they believe in it or not.

He once said, 'Arunachala is like a fire. If you go near it you will feel the heat whether you believe in it or not.'

I also heard him say once, 'If you go round this hill, it will give you its grace, even if you don't want it'.

Question: I read somewhere that Bhagavan said that *jnanis* have the power to link the individual mind to the supreme Self.

Annamalai Swami: Yes. A big ship can carry many people to the other side of the ocean, and a small ship can carry only a few people.

Question: And some *jnanis* don't carry anyone at all.

Annamalai Swami: These *jnanis* who don't have disciples don't appear to be helping anyone, but their power, the power of their realisation, is having a beneficial effect on all beings. It is true, though, that some *jnanis* pass away without teaching anyone directly. Lakshmi the cow and Bhagavan's mother are examples of this.

Question: Bhagavan once said that one *jnani* living on this earth is a tremendous help to all people.

Annamalai Swami: Yes, yes.

10

Question: I want to ask Swamiji about his own experience. Was his own experience a single event, an explosion of knowledge? Or did it happen more gradually, in a more subtle way?

Annamalai Swami: It was my experience that through continuous *sadhana* I gradually relaxed into the Self. It was a gradual process.

Question: So it is not necessarily something that happens with a big bang?

Annamalai Swami: It is not something new that suddenly comes. It is eternally there, but it is covered by so much. It has to be rediscovered.

Question: But do some people explode into That? I was with a man this morning who claims to be realised. He came here. Do you remember him? He said he had an experience of exploding into it, and that the experience of the Self, he says, stayed with him ever since 1982.

Annamalai Swami [laughing]: If he says, 'I don't know myself' or if he claims, 'I have known myself,' both are statements to laugh at. Because you *are* That. You can be That, but there is nothing to say about it. If somebody says, 'I am a *jnani*. I am an enlightened person,' then who is claiming that?

Question: Yes, exactly. Very good. Can I ask another question about my enquiry? I have been having small little glimpses, especially during sleep, of having no thoughts. There have been other glimpses in the most unlikely places. In Lucknow, which is a big, busy city, with people yelling and screaming everywhere, I was cycling down a crowded street when I suddenly felt the peace of the Self that was underlying everything. I could feel the Self, or at least it was an experience that I thought must have been the Self. There was a stillness and a silence in the midst of these utterly chaotic conditions. At other times the pendulum swings the other way and I feel completely lost in my mental world, and in the chaotic outside world.

I feel a little confusion about the process and the technique of self-enquiry, so much so I have to go back to reading Ramana's teachings on the subject again and again until the confusion leaves me. I would like Swami's comments on this. I know that there is nothing new that he can say about it. I know that I have to continue with self-enquiry.

Annamalai Swami: Constant meditation is the only way. If you bring the light into your room, the darkness immediately goes away. You have to see that the light is not put out. It has to be continuously burning so that there is no darkness. Until you get firmly established in the Self, you have to continue with your meditation. Doubts take possession of you only if you forget yourself.

Question: My doubts are not my only problem. I find that my yearning for the Self is not very strong. This bothers me quite a lot.

Annamalai Swami: When you forget the state of being yourself, then is the time to enquire, 'Who forgets the Self? Who is in doubt? Who is having the confusion?' Enquire in this way. Discard all that is not you and come back to yourself.

Question: Sometimes I am overpowered by self-doubt.

Annamalai Swami: If the meditation is not continuous enough, the other part of the mind becomes predominant. You have to overpower this mind that is taking you away from yourself by repeatedly doing this self-enquiry.

When you churn curd and separate butter and buttermilk, they will not become one again after they have been separated. If you take milk from the cow's udder, it will never go back into the cow again. In the same way, if you become established in the Self, you will never go back into ignorance again.

Question: When I do have these self doubts, the yearning or the desire to know myself does come up quite strongly, but at other times it is not there so strongly. What do you think about this?

Annamalai Swami: Whatever may be happening, enquire, 'To whom is all this happening?' Do this and go back to your Self, which is peace.

Question: I thought that this yearning was a plus point in my favour. Isn't it a help to have this yearning?

Annamalai Swami: If the intensity to know yourself is strong enough, the intensity of your yearning will take you to the Self.

Question: But still, I must keep up with the enquiry.

Annamalai Swami: If you remain in the Self, enquiry will not be necessary. If you move away from the Self and go back to the mind, you then have to enquire again and go back to your Self.

Question: To whom does this intensity to realise the Self arise? It has to arise to the 'I' that ultimately has to disappear.

Annamalai Swami: Who is this 'I'? It is neither the body nor the mind. If you remain as the Self, there is neither body nor mind. So what is this 'I'? Enquire into it and find out for yourself.

When you see the rope, what happens to the snake? Nothing happens to it because there never was a snake. Similarly, when you remain as the Self, there is a knowing that this 'I' never had any existence.

All is the Self. You are not separate from the Self. All is you. Your real state is the Self, and in that Self there is no body and no mind. This is the truth, and you know it by being it. This 'I am the body' idea is wrong. This false idea must go and the conviction 'I am the Self' should come to the extent that it becomes constant.

At the moment this 'I am the body' idea seems very natural for you. You should work towards the point where 'I am the Self' becomes natural to you. It happens when the wrong idea of being the body goes, and when you stop believing it to be true, it vanishes as darkness vanishes when the sun appears.

This life is all a dream, a dream within a dream within a dream. We dream this world, we dream that we die and take birth in another body. And in this birth we dream that we have dreams. All kinds of pleasures and suffering alternate in these dreams, but a moment comes when waking up happens. In this moment, which we call realising the Self, there is the understanding that all the births, all the deaths, all the sufferings and all the pleasures were unreal dreams that have finally come to an end.

Everyone has experienced dreams within dreams. One may dream that one has woken up from a dream, but that waking up is still happening within a dream. Our whole lives are dreams. When this dream life ends and a new one begins, there is no knowledge that both dreams are happening in the underlying dream of *samsara*.

Bhagavan has instructed us in *Who Am I?* to see the whole world as a dream. When realisation comes, nothing will affect you because you will have the firm knowledge that all manifestation is an unreal dream.

11

Question: When I was in Germany I used to meditate in front of Bhagavan's picture and feel very peaceful. One day, while I was sitting as usual in front of Bhagavan's picture, a light started emerging from the eyes of Bhagavan. It flowed out of the photo and embraced me. Soon afterwards I went into a peaceful, blissful, timeless state that I had never experienced before. I totally forgot about my body, time and my surroundings. There was only peace and consciousness. That experience made such a deep impression on me, it created a strong yearning in me to regain the experience. But I never got it back. No matter how much I try, I never feel that I am getting any closer to it. How can I get this experience back?

Annamalai Swami: By constant self-enquiry. 'Who had the experience, and who lost it? Who has the yearning to regain it? Who has all these thoughts about it?' If you follow this approach, you will ultimately realise who you really are.

The experience you had didn't come from somewhere else. It is already within you. Find out who had the experience.

Question: In order to do self-enquiry we have to use the mind, which is mostly troublesome and in reality does not even exist. Why is this?

Annamalai Swami: The mind that we use for self-enquiry is the pure mind, the sattvic mind. By using this sattvic mind we do self-enquiry to remove the impure mind, which is *rajas* and *tamas*. If you keep on doing self-enquiry with the sattvic mind, ultimately, this sattvic mind will be dissolved in the Self.

Question: Some time ago I felt very depressed and couldn't get out of this state. One day while I was doing *giri pradakshina*, which I do every day, I stopped on Bhagavan's bridge [the parapet wall of a culvert about four miles from Ramanasramam] and started meditating on Arunachala with closed eyes. Suddenly the depression lifted and was replaced by peace. This depression has not returned.

Annamalai Swami: The one who had the depression was not you. Your real nature is peace. Don't identify yourself with either the mind or with the depressed states it produces. These are not you.

Question: After this depression left me, I found that I was always in a peaceful state. Soon afterwards I met an Indian girl and fell in love with her. Sometimes the thought arises that I would like to marry this girl. Is it advisable to get married? Would it not be a hindrance to my *sadhana*?

Annamalai Swami: Is this girl spiritually oriented?

Question: Yes, she often goes to temples and reads spiritual books.

Annamalai Swami: If the partner has progressed spiritually to the same extent that you have, it would be a great help. But if one partner is less interested in spiritual matters than the other, the one who has less interest will drag the other down, unless the more interested partner is spiritually very powerful. And in such a situation there would always be quarrels and tension. If both partners have the same spiritual yearnings to realise the Self, married life is OK. Otherwise it is a hindrance.

Question: How can we keep up our *sadhana* in the middle of all our daily activities? It is very difficult.

Annamalai Swami: Ramakrishna was once asked this question, and in reply he gave the example of a child who was playing by spinning round and round. If you do this you will soon get dizzy and fall over, but if the same child spins round and round while holding firmly onto a post at arm's length, the child's grip on the post will keep him upright and prevent him from falling over. In this dizzy, spinning world of *samsara*, if you hold onto the post of the Self, you will be able to stay upright and not fall over.

I can give you another example. When you cut jackfruits open with your bare hands, there is an unpleasant, milky liquid inside that sticks to your fingers and makes it very hard to take out the fruit. And afterwards it takes hours to scrub it all off. However, if you put a little oil on your fingers before you start the work, this milky liquid will not bother you because it cannot stick to your oiled hands.

Without some protection, contact with worldly matters can prove to be sticky and unpleasant. But if you oil yourself with remembrance of the Self, you can move smoothly and efficiently through the world, without having any of your business affairs stick to you or cause you any trouble or inconvenience. When there is a remembrance of the

Self, everything in life proceeds smoothly, and there is no attachment to the work that is being done.

Question: While you were doing a lot of work in the ashram, how did you manage to keep up your *sadhana*?

Annamalai Swami: In those days Bhagavan was accessible for most of the time, so I was able to get regular guidance in my *sadhana*. He told me to read *Sivananda Lahari, Ellam Ondre, Upadesa Saram* and his other writings. He also told me to do *parayana* [chanting of scriptural works]. All this was very helpful in keeping my mind on the Self during work.

Sri Bhagavan often said, 'While doing the work, don't have the idea, "I am doing the work". If you can keep up this attitude, work will not be a burden, and no problems will touch you.'

Don't differentiate between work and meditation. If you don't differentiate, every job you do becomes meditation. And don't make distinctions between different kinds of work. Don't think, 'This is good work. That is bad work.' If you treat all work equally, any work you do will be beneficial for your *sadhana*.

Question: We have to live in the world and deal with people, many of whom will try to take advantage of us. Being quiet and detached is one thing, but should we be so quiet and uninterested that we allow other people to take advantage of our passivity?

Annamalai Swami: You can be quiet within and be tough on the outside, if that is the role you have to play in the world.

There is a story about a snake that lived under a bush by the side of the street. Whenever people passed the bush, the snake made a lot of noise and tried to bite them. It gave a lot of trouble to anyone who came near.

One day a wandering *sadhu* passed the bush and the snake, as usual, put on an aggressive show of behaviour.

The *sadhu*, who could communicate with animals, said, 'Keep quiet and don't bite people. You don't have to behave like this. Live a peaceful life and don't trouble the people who walk past.'

The snake heeded the advice and from that day on its behaviour completely changed. It sat quietly under its bush and never troubled any of the people who walked past.

Within a few days the local people realised that the snake was no longer a threat to them, but instead of being relieved, they would throw stones at the snake, or try to chase it away. People have this instinctive response to snakes. Whenever they see one, they feel compelled to commit some act of violence against it. The snake ignored the provocation for a while but it soon realised that this new state of affairs was not an improvement on the previous one.

A few days later the *sadhu* came by and asked how the snake's new lifestyle was going.

'Not so good,' responded the snake. 'I am suffering a lot on account of your advice. I am being very calm and I am not giving any trouble to anyone, but because of my calmness and *sadhu*-like behaviour, people are taking advantage of me by throwing stones at me and harassing me. They would never do this before because they knew I might retaliate and bite them.'

The *sadhu* thought about this for some time and then spoke.

'I advised you to be calm and not trouble anyone, but that doesn't mean that you have to sit here passively while people come along and hurt you. When people come to cause you trouble in future, just pretend that you are going to bite them. You can be angry on the outside, but on the inside you can still be calm.'

From then on the snake adopted the new tactic of hissing at everyone who came past his bush, just to let them know that he was still a potential threat. This was enough to make people give him a wide berth.

We can all be like this if circumstances demand it. There are occasions when a show of anger is needed. We can play the role of being angry, but at the same time we can know that we are just acting out a role that is needed at a particular moment. Internally we can be peaceful while all this is going on.

12

Annamalai Swami: *Jnanis* usually come to their last births with a mountain of *punyas* on account of what they have done in their previous lives. The *jnani* cannot experience all these *punyas* himself, but those who come into contact with him can receive them as blessings. The same thing can be said for all the *papams* that the *jnani* brings to his final life.

A poor man can suddenly become rich if a millionaire takes a liking to him and gives him a lot of money. Those who come to a *jnani* and do selfless service to him find themselves becoming spiritual millionaires when they receive the *jnani's* unused *punyas*. And those who come to abuse and insult the *jnani* end up receiving all his unused *papams*. This is an automatic process. The *jnani* does not pick and choose the people who are going to be the recipients of these *punyas*. This transfer happens automatically. Devotees grow spiritually by receiving all these blessings. They reach heights that would be difficult or impossible to reach through their own efforts.

My own life illustrates this. When I was very young I stayed alone, doing all kinds of spiritual practice by myself. I doubt that I could have experienced the truth of the Self through my own efforts. Fortunately, grace brought me to Bhagavan, and through Bhagavan's grace I had the opportunity to serve him. My proximity to Bhagavan and the work I did for him made me ready for the truth.

I learned this lesson about the necessity of being in the *jnani's* presence early on in my time at Ramanasramam. After a few weeks there I found myself disappointed by the attitude of many of the people I found around Bhagavan. They seemed to be more interested in gossiping than in doing meditation. I knew that Bhagavan was a great man, but I didn't feel comfortable living with people whom I thought were not taking the spiritual life very seriously. I decided to leave the ashram and meditate by myself. My attempt to run away was not successful. Bhagavan's grace and power brought me back from Polur, the place I had run away to. As I sat in front of Bhagavan on my first day back, Bhagavan looked at me, and while he was looking I began to hear the words of one of the verses from *Ulladu Narpadu Anubandham* resonating in my Heart:

'The supreme state which is praised and which is attained here in this life by clear enquiry, which rises in the Heart when association with a *sadhu* is gained, is impossible to attain by listening to preachers, by studying and learning the meaning of the scriptures, by virtuous deeds, or by any other means.'

I had never read this work before, so I don't know how these words managed to repeat themselves inside me. No one else heard them except me. The verse praises association with a *jnani*, saying that association with such a being is far more productive for *sadhaks* than doing spiritual practice by oneself. After hearing these words I got the courage to stay on at Ramanasramam and serve Bhagavan.

Question: You said that by serving a *jnani* one could receive his unused *punyas* as a blessing. Does one not need a lot of *punyas* of one's own merely to have the opportunity to meet a *jnani* and serve him? It's not just a question of good luck.

Annamalai Swami: Yes. One of our saints has written a verse to this effect: 'Those who have accumulated *punyas* in many lives, those who have purified their minds to some extent, those who have made a big spiritual effort over many lives – these kinds of virtuous souls will get association with a realised Guru, and by his grace they will come to realise the truth.'

If you want to get hot, you have to go near a fire. If you want water, you have to go to a well, and if you want grace to realise the Self, you will have to go to a *jnani*.

Bhagavan would occasionally quote a verse from *Kaivalya Navaneeta* that says: 'The immemorial *Vedas* declare that single-minded devotion to a holy sage is not only pleasing to Brahma, Vishnu and Siva together, but also secures the rewards of all the vedic rites, and finally, liberation from the cycle of births.'

After my first attempt to run away, I never left Bhagavan again. I never went anywhere else to do my spiritual practices. I just listened to what my Guru told me, and I carried out his instructions to the best of my ability.

Then, one day in the hall, Bhagavan turned to me and said, 'Your *karmas* are over'.

I had this great opportunity to surrender to a Guru like Bhagavan, to trust him and to serve him. It didn't happen through my own efforts. This kind of thing happens very rarely, for beings such as Bhagavan don't appear very often. If you want to learn, you have to go to school. If you want *jnana*, you have to go to a *jnani*.

I want to speak some more about the grace of the Guru. Bhagavan told me that the Guru is the Self who is within. The Self manifests in a form and pushes the minds of devotees towards the Self. At the same time the Guru resides within us as the unmanifest Self. From the inside, he is pulling us towards him. This pushing and pulling is the Guru's grace.

For the Guru's grace to work on us, we have to surrender. We have to give up all the things of this world, and all other worlds, and direct all our attention towards the Self. If we want anything in this world or the next, our energy will be dispersed in these desires, and to fulfil these desires we shall have to be born again and again.

I once told Bhagavan that I had a desire to go and live in a cave where I could do meditation by myself.

Bhagavan told me, 'If you keep a desire like that in your mind, you will have to take one more birth. Why keep such a desire? If it is destined for you, it will happen by itself. Leave this idea alone.'

So, give up all your desires, your likes, dislikes and preferences. If you are truly the whole, which part of yourself will you like or dislike?

To strengthen my resolve Bhagavan would sometimes tell me inspiring stories of service and devotion from the lives of other great teachers. He twice told me about Virupakshadeva and Guhai Namasivaya, two great beings who lived on Arunachala several centuries ago.

These two served their Guru in Karnataka very faithfully for many years. At the end of this period the Guru sent both of them to Arunachala and told them to meditate there. They came here and picked different spots for their *tapas*: Virupaksha Deva sat in the cave that is now named after him, and Guhai Namasivaya picked a cave that was further down the hill. They both attained liberation after years of meditating here. Eventually, they attracted devotees of their own and started ashrams here.

Perhaps Bhagavan told me this story because he knew that it ʽwas my destiny to be sent to meditate by myself after many years of service.

If a disciple serves a Guru, the Guru does not gain anything from it, but the disciple, by his service, becomes purified and fit to receive the truth. A ship may be taking you to the other shore of the ocean, but the ship itself is not gaining anything from you.

There is one more verse that I want to quote for you. It was sung by Manikkavachagar whose supreme devotion to Siva enabled him to realise the Self. Bhagavan often quoted Manikkavachagar's poems to us.

'I gave myself to you. In return, you must give yourself to me. So in this business of giving and taking, who is the real winner? In our transactions I received limitless *ananda* from you. But what did you get from me? Nothing! Just a useless ego. So now you are residing in my Heart. What more do I need? I have become fulfilled. I need nothing because you are in my Heart.'

Manikkavachagar could sing like this because Siva himself was residing within him as his own reality. His desires were fulfilled. He needed nothing.

13

Annamalai Swami: In the 1930s I received a telegram stating that my father had passed away.

I reported the fact to Bhagavan and asked, 'Please give him *moksha* [liberation]'.

Bhagavan nodded and said 'Yes'.

Soon afterwards Chinnaswami asked me to take a bath because, in our Hindu tradition, when either our father or mother dies, we have to take a purificatory bath.

I told Chinnaswami, 'My father has not died. Bhagavan is my father. He is still here. The man who has just died was the father in my last birth. My father in this birth is Bhagavan, my Guru. I don't need to take a bath.'

There is another Hindu tradition surrounding death. If anyone dies in the family, we don't take food until the body has been disposed of. When Bhagavan's mother died at Skandashram, Bhagavan ignored this rule, saying, 'Mother is not dead. Let us eat.'

In this case there was no ritual pollution involved because his mother had realised the Self in her final moments. In such circumstances, the usual rules on bathing and fasting do not apply.

There were other Hindu dietary rules that Bhagavan sometimes ignored. When there is a solar or lunar eclipse, we are not supposed to cook or eat.

On one such occasion Bhagavan said, 'Come on, let us take our food as usual. We don't have to worry about this eclipse.'

Some of the brahmins, who were more strict about obeying these sorts of rules, were afraid to break their lifetime habits, but the rest of us went with Bhagavan and ate our food with him.

After Bhagavan's mother died in 1922 Bhagavan continued to live at Skandashram for several months. Then, one day, he went down the hill to his mother's *samadhi* and stayed there. Some power, some *shakti*, compelled him to go down the hill and abandon Skandashram. Soon afterwards Skandashram was robbed and the thieves took cooking pots and a few other things away. Up till then some of the devotees had been staying at Skandashram to guard the place and the few things that were left there, but after this theft, it was more or less abandoned and everyone moved down the hill and stayed there. Many people came to serve Bhagavan food there, and the items that were lost were soon replaced by donations from the visiting devotees.

In the beginning it was very primitive. Everyone, including

Bhagavan, slept outside by a mango tree. The first building was a mud hut with a thatched roof that was erected over the site of Mother's *samadhi*. I came along a few years later, at a time when the ashram was beginning to expand and put up new buildings. All these buildings were erected on the basis of plans that had been drawn up by Bhagavan.

In those days cement was not available and we had to use a mortar made out of lime. I was very sensitive to the chemicals in this mixture. I was always getting allergic reactions to them. Every morning I would wake up with puss oozing out of my eyes. I had to work outside in the heat all day and my body felt like it was overheating even during the cool of the evenings. Bhagavan taught me how to prepare a special mixture made out of coconut oil, sesame oil and castor oil. He told me that if I applied this mixture to my feet in the evening, it would take away this feeling of overheating. I tried it and it worked very well. Up till then I had found it hard to sleep at night on account of this feeling of heat that was always in my body. After I started applying this mixture, I always had a good night's sleep.

At some point while I was serving Bhagavan the ashram acquired the house in Tiruchuzhi where Bhagavan was born. Chinnaswami asked me to go there and do some construction work on the old house. He wanted to turn it into some kind of temple.

I didn't want to leave Bhagavan so I told Chinnaswami, 'I have completed all my temple worshipping and my bathing in holy waters in my previous births. That's why I have come to Bhagavan now. I don't need these activities any more.'

Chinnaswami didn't pursue this matter with me and I never went to Tiruchuzhi.

I had enough *punyas* to come to Bhagavan and receive his grace because I had done all these things in other lives. The charitable works, the good actions, the temple rituals, etc. that I had done in past lives earned me the right to come to Bhagavan's presence, to stay there and serve him. They had served their purpose and I didn't need them any more. All these ritual activities lost their appeal for me within a few days of encountering Bhagavan and his teachings.

Question: In Swamiji's book I read that he liked to drink the water that had been left in Bhagavan's cup. This is some kind of ritual that he persisted with long after he came to Ramanasramam. Does Swamiji make a distinction between ordinary rituals and accepting leftovers from the Guru?

Annamalai Swami: When I worked in the ashram I used to drink the water with which Bhagavan had washed his hands. I would get this water two or three times a day. Even after I moved to Palakottu, I still occasionally drank this water because Mudaliar Patti sometimes used to bring it to me. She knew that I liked this water, and she knew that I had been accustomed to drinking it.

Sundaram [translator]: I once asked Swamiji why he was so attached to drinking this water. He said that it was on account of a story he had read when he was still living in his village. The story was about a sage called Pattinathar who lived with his disciple Badragiriyar in a village called Tiruvidaimarudur.

Annamalai Swami [continuing the story]: Every day these two used to give their leftover food to a dog. Sometime later this dog died and took birth as a princess in the household of the king of Benares. When she grew up, the king wanted to arrange her marriage, but she refused, saying that instead of marrying, she wanted to see a sage called Pattinathar who lived in Tiruvidaimarudur. Seeing how determined she was, the king himself agreed to take her to see this man. As soon as she arrived there, Pattinathar recognised her and told his disciple that in her previous life she had been the dog that had been given their leftover food.

Then Pattinathar added, 'She will become enlightened because she ate that food'.

The disciple found this whole story hard to believe.

'How can a dog take birth as a human being?' he asked. 'And how can she get enlightened merely on account of having eaten this food?'

Pattinathar answered, 'I will show you,' and then proceeded to walk to a nearby Siva temple. The princess and the disciple followed.

As they stood together inside the temple, Siva appeared in front of them in the form of light. The light engulfed both the disciple and the princess and absorbed them into itself. Pattinathar was left standing alone.

He asked Siva, 'I am all alone in this world now. Please tell me how I can also merge with you.'

Siva replied, 'Take this bitter-tasting sugarcane with you and visit my temples. Each time you visit a temple, taste the sugarcane. If it tastes very sweet, there, in that temple, you will attain *samadhi* and become one with me.'

Pattinathar followed these instructions and visited many temples, but during this period, which lasted many years, each time he tasted the sugarcane in these places, it always tasted bitter. Finally, he arrived at Tiruvantiyar, a small town near Madras. He bit into the sugarcane, and in the moment that its sweet taste touched his tongue, he attained *mahasamadhi* and physically disappeared.

It was the memory of this story that made me want to drink Bhagavan's leftover water.

In the 1930's, while I was still serving Bhagavan in the ashram, I developed a severe stomach ache. One of Bhagavan's doctor-devotees decided to take me to Madras for a check up. I was examined there but the cause of the stomach ache was not found. As I was about to return to the ashram, I remembered this story of Pattinathar and decided to visit the temple at Tiruvantiyar on my way home. I had heard from other people that when Pattinathar dematerialised in that temple, he left a Siva *lingam* behind. When I went to pay homage to him in his *samadhi* temple, I saw that this *lingam* was still there.

14

Question: During deep meditation peace is there all the time. But there is still a feeling that peace is something that can come and go. I know that this is just an idea, but I want to eliminate this idea and have the direct experience of the peace that never comes and goes.

Bhagavan says, 'You are always the Self. It is just your notion that you are not the Self that has to be got rid of.' How does this happen?

Annamalai Swami: The Self is peace and happiness. Realising peace and happiness within you is the true realisation of the Self. You cannot distinguish between peace, happiness and the Self. They are not separate aspects. You have this idea that peace and happiness is within you, so you make some effort to find it there, but at the moment it is still only an idea for you.

So, ask yourself, 'To whom does this idea come? Who has this idea?'

You must pursue this line if you want to have the idea replaced by the experience. Peace is not an idea, nor is it something that comes and goes. We are always That. So, remain as That. You have no birth and no death, no bondage and no freedom. It is perpetual peace, and it is free from all ideas. The 'I am the body' idea is what is concealing it. This is what has to go.

Question: So the notion of being the body and the mind comes back and covers the experience?

Annamalai Swami: Yes, yes. This idea, 'I am the body,' is not there during sleep. Everyone enjoys sleeping, and the reason we enjoy it is because there are no thoughts there. It is the thoughts that arise subsequently that cause us all our trouble. There is no separate entity during sleep because no thought has arisen to create the image of one. When waking comes, this first rising thought, 'I am the body,' brings separation, doubts and confusion. If you can be without it in the waking state there will be the knowledge, 'I am Ramana, I am Arunachala. Everything is myself.' Ram, Krishna, etc., are all you. It is just this limiting 'I am the body' thought that keeps this knowledge, this awareness from you.

In the waking state, the *jnani* has no limiting thoughts, no ego that identifies with a name and a form. His state is crystal clear.

Ramana Bhagavan had no ego, no limiting thoughts, which is why he knew himself to be this peace, this happiness.

Question: How can we avoid getting attached to the form of the Guru, to his personality, and to the place where the Guru lives?

Annamalai Swami: If you completely avoid attachment to your body and mind, then all other attachments will vanish. Identify with That which is neither body nor mind, and all your attachments will go. You can only put your attention on one thing at a time. While it is on the mind or the body, it cannot be on the Self. Conversely, if you put attention on the Self and become absorbed in it, there will be no awareness of mind and body.

Every night during sleep you let go of your attachment to both the body and the mind, and the result is silence, peace, and an absence of duality. You can have this silence, this peace, and this absence of duality in the waking state by not believing the rising thoughts that create duality for you. Resist limiting thoughts. Replace them with thoughts such as 'All is myself. Everybody is myself. All animals, all things are myself.' What you think, you become. If you understand and experience that everything is yourself, how can you have likes and dislikes? If everything is you, there will be no desire to avoid anything, no impulse to discriminate in favour of anything.

If you want to discriminate at all, avoid bad company and bad thoughts. At night, when you suddenly start to experience the cold, you pull a blanket over yourself. Pull the blanket of discrimination over yourself when you feel that there is a possibility of bad company and bad thoughts dragging you down.

You may need to do this but the *jnani* will not because nothing can ever drag him back into the realm of false identifications again. He will always be in that state in which he knows everything to be himself. He will never again have the idea that anything is different or apart from his own Self.

67

15

Annamalai Swami: Bhagavan watched me very closely in the years that I served him in the ashram. One time I went to the Mother's temple where many people were talking about worldly matters.

Bhagavan called me back, saying, 'Why should you go to that crowd? Don't go to crowded places. If you move with the crowd, their *vasanas* will infect you.'

Bhagavan always encouraged me to live a solitary life and not mix with other people. That was the path he picked for me. Other people got different advice that was equally good for them. But while he actively discouraged me from socialising, he also discouraged me from sitting quietly and meditating during the years that I was working in the ashram. In this period of my life, if Bhagavan saw me sitting with my eyes closed he would call out to me and give me some work to do.

On one of these occasions he told me, 'Don't sit and meditate. It will be enough if you don't forget that you are the Self. Keep this in your mind all the time while you are working. This *sadhana* will be enough for you. The real *sadhana* is not to forget the Self. It is not sitting quietly with one's eyes closed. You are always the Self. Just don't forget it.'

Bhagavan's way does not create a war between the mind and the body. He does not make people sit down and fight the mind with closed eyes. Usually, when you sit in meditation, you are struggling to achieve something, fighting to gain control over the mind. Bhagavan did not advise us to engage in this kind of fight. He told us that there is no need to engage in a war against the mind, because mind does not have any real, fundamental existence. This mind, he said, is nothing but a shadow. He advised me to be continuously aware of the Self while I did the ordinary things of everyday life, and in my case, this was enough.

If you understand the Self and be that Self, everything will appear to you as your own Self. No problems will ever come to you while you have this vision. Because you are all and all is the Self, choices about liking or disliking will not arise. If you put on green-tinted glasses, everything you see will appear to be green. If you adopt the vision of the Self, everything that is seen will be Self and Self alone.

So these were Bhagavan's teachings for me: 'If you want to understand the Self, no formal *sadhana* is required. You are always the Self. Be aware of the Self while you are working. Convince yourself that you are the Self, and not the body or the mind, and always avoid the thought, "I am not the Self". '

Avoid thoughts that limit you, thoughts that make you believe that you are not the Self.

I once asked Bhagavan: 'You are at the top of the hill. You have reached the summit of spiritual life, whereas I am still at the bottom of the hill. Please help me to reach the summit.'

Bhagavan answered, 'It will be enough if you give up the thought, "I am at the bottom of the hill". If you can do this, there will be no difference between us. It is just your thoughts that are convincing you that I am at the top and you are at the bottom. If you can give up this difference, you will be fine.'

Don't adopt attitudes such as these that automatically assume that you are limited or inferior in any way.

On another occasion I asked Bhagavan: 'Nowadays, many people are crossing big oceans by plane in very short periods of time. I would like Bhagavan to find us a good device, a *jnana* airplane that can speedily transport us all to *moksha*.'

This time Bhagavan replied, 'We are both travelling in a *jnana* airplane, but you don't understand this.'

In his answers to me Bhagavan would never let me fall into the false belief that I was separate or different from him, or that I was a person with a mind and a body who needed to do something to reach some exalted spiritual state. Whenever I asked him questions that were based on assumptions such as these, he would show me the error that was implicit in the question and gently point me back to the truth, the Self. He would never allow me to entertain wrong ideas.

Question: What other questions did Swamiji ask during his early days at Ramanasramam?

Annamalai Swami: When I first came to Bhagavan I used to ask questions about liberation. What is bondage? What is freedom? And so on.

Muruganar, who was sitting next to me on one of these occasions, laughed and said, 'This boy doesn't even know what liberation is and what bondage is'.

I think he was amused by the innocence of my enquiries. After I began serving Bhagavan, I listened very attentively to all the philosophical explanations that he gave. I also talked to Chadwick and other devotees about various aspects of Vedanta. I gradually absorbed the teachings until a point came where I could say that I had a good working knowledge of Bhagavan's teachings and the various other systems that were being discussed in his presence.

In one of his later songs Muruganar wrote about Bhagavan, 'You make wise people of those who come to you in an ignorant state. This is the grace of Ramana.'

I always felt that this was a reference to me.

It wasn't easy in the beginning. When I first came to the ashram, I was so forgetful I rarely remembered anything that Bhagavan said. Because I was so forgetful, I used to keep a paper and pencil and write down whatever Bhagavan was saying.

I felt that my forgetfulness was a hindrance to absorbing Bhagavan's teachings, so one day I approached him and said, 'Bhagavan, my memory is very bad. Could you please bless me with a good one.'

Bhagavan looked into my eyes for a few minutes without saying anything. From that day on my memory became very clear and sharp, so much so, I gave up carrying my pencil and paper.

16

[A woman on a pilgrimage stopped off to visit Annamalai Swami and ask for his blessings and advice.]

Annamalai Swami: Don't forget your Self wherever you go. If you can manage this, you will not need anything else. A student once came to Bhagavan and told him that he wanted to go for further education. Bhagavan told him, 'This education is good for you. Study more. But at the same time study the person who is studying. Study yourself.' One of the old Siddhas [Tamil poet-saints who lived about 1,000 years ago] composed a song:

'I yearned for and searched for the truth. I ran everywhere looking for it. I wasted my life, my time and my energy looking everywhere for this truth. So much time was wasted in this pursuit, I have grown old and am about to die. But finally I have understood that the true light is within myself.'

You are going to different places on a pilgrimage, but what you are really looking for is you yourself. You cannot achieve success in this by going on external searches because you yourself are the one that is being looked for. Your real nature is peace. Forgetting this, you have lost your peace and you are searching in the outside world where there is no peace to be found.

This is the teaching of Bhagavan, my Guru. I am passing it on to you.

You must understand who you are and what you are, and then you must remain as that. If you can manage this, this itself will suffice. Right now you are under the impression that you are your body and your mind, but the truth is, you are the Self. Let go of the 'I' that you imagine yourself to be and catch hold of the real 'I', the Self.

What do you hope to gain from your pilgrimage, from going here and there in an external journey? You are holding onto the idea that you are your body and your mind. Having assumed this, you are now looking for an external God so that you can worship him. Though such worship may be beneficial, it will not take you beyond the realm of the mind. While you hold onto the idea that you are a person inside a body, whatever you see will be a manifestation of your own mind. You cannot transcend the mind by worshipping your own external projections. All these external appearances that you see in front of you are *maya*. They have no fundamental abiding reality. To find the Self, to find what is true and real, you have to look inside yourself. You have to find the source, the place where all these mental projections arise.

You are looking for satisfaction in the outside world because you think that all these objects you see in front of you are real. They are not. The reality is the substratum in which they all appear. This is what you should be seeking, instead of looking for external gods in different pilgrimage places.

An elephant is made out of wood. If we see it as wood, it is wood. But if we get caught up in the name and form, we will see only an elephant and forget that its underlying nature is wood.

All is your own Self. This form is different; that form is different. This is more powerful; this is worse. These are all judgements you make when you see separate objects instead of having the true vision that all is an undifferentiated oneness. There may be different varieties of light bulbs, but the current that activates and sustains them is the same. You must learn to become one with this activating current, the unmanifest Self, and not get caught up in all the names and forms that appear in it.

Here is another verse from one of the Siddhas:

'Because of your ego you are going to the forest to look for spiritual light. You are looking for this *darshan* of light in Badrinath and other Himalayan pilgrimage places. These things are the illusion of the mind. They depend on the states of the mind and the functioning of the mind. That which you are searching for is within yourself.'

Bhagavan wrote in *Ulladu Narpadu,* verse eleven: 'Knowing all else without knowing oneself, the knower of objects known, is nothing but ignorance. How instead can it be knowledge?'

All the information the mind accumulates and all the experiences it collects are ignorance, false knowledge. Real knowledge cannot be found in the mind or in any external location. The mind sees through coloured glasses, and what it sees is tinted and tainted by that colour. If your mind is in a spoiled and disturbed condition, the entire world will appear to be in a spoiled and disturbed condition. If your mind is crystal clear, everything will appear to you to be clear and peaceful.

Your most important objective must be realising the Self. If you have not done this, you will spend your time in ignorance and illusion. You, your mind, this world – they are all *maya.* Don't become a slave to this *maya.* Instead, realise the Self and let *maya* become your servant.

I have just remembered another verse from the Siddhas:

'Many people have struggled years together to realise the Self. Millions and millions of people have struggled, looking for the light outside themselves. If these millions and millions of people have died without understanding the Self that is within them, it is because they didn't understand the real path.'

You must find someone who has followed the right path, someone who has discovered this inner truth for himself, and who stabilised himself there. Such a one will give you good advice. He will not send you out on unproductive adventures in the outside world. Following the advice of someone who has not reached this state is simply a case of the blind leading the blind. Neither knows the right path and both will eventually fall into a big hole.

You may find a fruit that is very bitter and decide to improve its flavour. You could take it to all the holy rivers in the country and wash it in each one, but when you come home, the fruit will not be any less bitter than the day you started. You can carry your mind to every corner of the country, visiting all the famous pilgrimage places on the way, bathing in all the holy rivers, doing *pujas* at all the sacred shrines, but when you return your mind will be in the same state as the day you started. Mind is not improved by long journeys to far-flung places. Instead, make an internal pilgrimage. Take the mind back to its source and plunge it into the peace-giving waters of the Self. If you once make this pilgrimage, you will never need to go looking for happiness or peace in any other place.

Question: Is it not good to remember God and to repeat his name?

Annamalai Swami: The *Ribhu Gita* advises us to remember at all times, 'I am the Self; all is the Self'. The entire universe is 'I'. If you can keep this permanently in your mind, millions and millions of *punyas* will come to you. There were many books that Bhagavan liked, but *Ribhu Gita* was definitely one of the best. He once said that *Ribhu Gita* is a book for one's last life.

You must have read Hanuman's story in the *Ramayana*. Hanuman's mind was completely lost in the name of Ram, and because of this he accumulated great powers. He was able to jump across the ocean because of his full and complete devotion. I advise doing *japa* to the Self, either by repeatedly thinking about it or by repeating affirmations such as 'I am the Self'. This affirmation is the greatest mantra of all. If you can do it continuously, without interruption, you will get results very quickly. There is no greater *japa*, no greater *sadhana* than this.

The one who is seeking is also that which is sought. The seeker and the sought are both Self. If you are not able to find this Self within yourself, you will not find it anywhere else. Searching on the outside and visiting holy places will not help you.

Many people are visiting swamis, temples and holy places. Doing these things will not yield any good fruit. For real and lasting results you have to look inside yourself and discover the Self within. You can do that anywhere.

Question: Many people say that they have found peace in holy places.

Annamalai Swami: If you are attached to places, stay here in Tiruvannamalai for some time. The best place to discover the Self is here at Arunachala. The power to know the Self is available here. That has been the experience of many sages, including Bhagavan. Arunachala is the Self. Ramana is the Self. Both are here. Both are inside you.

You have an inclination towards holy places. Try this one for some time, and don't be so keen to rush off to other places.

Keep up the meditation, 'I am the Self,' and be completely surrendered to that Self that is within you and which has appeared here in the forms of Bhagavan and Arunachala. Forget about your bus for a while.

Question: I am now wondering if I should cancel this trip. I am having strong doubts as to whether I should leave or not.

Annamalai Swami: You have to make that decision for yourself. I have given you my advice. Now, you have to decide for yourself whether you are going to act on it. All I will say is that wherever you go in life, don't forget yourself.

Question: If I do go, I will be back in a maximum of twelve days.

Annamalai Swami: Turn to the light within all the time.

Question: Thank you, Swami.

Annamalai Swami [laughing]: It's your destiny to leave. That's why you have to go. But you are still having some doubts as to whether this has really been decided or not. Don't indulge in them. Do what you have to do and remember the Self at all times.

17

Annamalai Swami: You stumble around in the darkness of your mind, not knowing that you have a torch in your hand. That light is the light of the Self. Switch it on and leave it on and you will never stumble again.

You are all here because there is a desire in you to realise the Self. This desire does not arise randomly or accidentally in some people and not in others. It is there because of the *punyas* you have accumulated from previous births, *punyas* that may have come from meditation, charitable works, and so on. These *punyas* will manifest as a desire for freedom, a desire to do earnest *sadhana*, a desire to find a good teacher in whose presence the truth will be taught and revealed. If someone is destined to be a *jnani* in this life, it means that he has come to this final birth with a mountain of *punyas* to his credit. These *punyas* will take him to a real Guru, to a real *satsang*, and in this environment he will do *sadhana* and achieve the goal.

If one does not have this mountain of *punyas* from the past, there will be no desire for freedom, no desire to look for a Guru who can deliver it. Such a person may meet a Guru and that Guru may even give him good advice, but the determined resolve to put that advice into effect will not be there. The fierce determination to succeed and the discrimination that allows one to ignore worldly entanglements only arise in those who have accumulated these *punyas*. Other people may hear the words of truth, but although they accept that they are true, the inclination to act on them will not be there.

Wet wood does not catch fire easily, but if you dry it for a long time in the sun it will be much more combustible. Other materials such as camphor, petrol, kerosene and gunpowder will ignite as soon as they are touched by a flame. Devotees can be classified in the same way: some ignite as soon as they meet a Guru or hear the truth for the first time; others need a period of drying out before they are ready to catch fire.

Those who are damp or wet can dry themselves out by *sadhana*, by having a strong determination to be aware of the Self at all times. Self is readily available all the time but we cannot be aware of it or even put our attention on the thought of it because our *vasanas* are continuously leading our interest and attention in other directions. That is why it is so important to have the awareness, 'I am not the mind. I am the Self.' You have forcibly to drag your wandering attention back to the Self each time it shows an interest in going anywhere else. Don't be interested in the words that the mind is serving up for you. It is putting them there to tempt you into a stream of thoughts that will take you away from the Self. You have to ignore them all and focus on the light that is shining within you.

When I was serving Bhagavan in the 1930s and 40s, I obeyed only him. For me, he was the light, and everything else was the chattering mind trying to lead me astray. I ignored the words and advice of everyone else in the ashram and kept all my attention on Bhagavan and his instructions to me. Even Chinnaswami had to concede, finally, that I was following the correct course.

One day he came up to me and said, 'You are not listening to my words or carrying out my instructions. You are only paying attention to Bhagavan's orders. This determination could only be a result of all the *punyas* you have accumulated in many previous lives.'

If there is no external light such as Bhagavan to guide you, you have to look within to find the Self. You will not benefit from looking anywhere else, from doing anything else, or from listening to any other voice. Walking round and round a temple, doing rituals to a deity – activities like these will not bring you any nearer to the Self. The *pujas*, the *japas*, the rituals – these are just for beginners. Meditation is the syllabus in a higher class. We need not waste our time by indulging in the activities of the infant class again and again. Here, in this class, I ask you to put all your attention, all your interest on realising the final teaching: 'I am not the body or the mind. I am Self. All is the Self.' This is Bhagavan's final teaching. Nothing more needs to be added to it. Keep good company while you pursue this knowledge and all will be well.

Question: I know that listening to the Guru and believing his words is important. When he says, 'You are the Self. The world is not real,' and so on, I can accept that what he says is true, but my belief in the truth of those words doesn't seem to make it my experience.

Annamalai Swami: You must believe the Guru and you must also believe your own experience because the Guru is not telling you to add another belief to your mind. He is instead telling you to look at your own experience of yourself, and in doing so, disregard everything else.

There is a story that Ram Tirtha used to tell. A man who was a little mad lived in a small village with his wife. His friends liked to tease him and make fun of him because they all thought he was stupid.

One day, one of them said, 'We have some bad news for you. Your wife has become a widow.'

He believed them and started crying out in grief, 'My wife has become a widow! My wife has become a widow!'

Some of the people he passed on the street laughed at him and said, 'Why are you mourning? You are very much alive. How can your wife be a widow if you yourself are alive to complain about it?'

'My closest friends have told me this,' he replied, 'and I trust them. They are very reliable people. If they are saying that my wife has become a widow, it must be true.'

We would think that a man who behaved like this was utterly stupid because he chose to believe the words of others instead of his own experience. But are we any better? We believe, on the basis of indirect information provided by the senses, that we are the body. The experience of 'I am', of the Self, is present in all of us, but when the mischievous senses gang up on us and try to make us believe something that is patently untrue, we believe them and ignore our direct experience.

Then we grieve about our state, lamenting, 'I am bound; I am unenlightened; I am not free'.

And even when the Guru comes along and says, 'You are the Self. You are free. Why do you insist on believing this misinformation that the mischievous senses are giving you?' Still you do not believe the truth.

You tell him, 'The senses have always given me reliable information in the past. I have learned to trust them. What they tell me must be true.'

And so you go on grieving and complaining, even when your direct experience and the words of the Guru agree with each other and reveal the truth.

Question: You are saying that I should listen to the Guru because what he says is the truth of who I am?

Annamalai Swami: You should trust the Guru because his interest is in showing you the truth. He may occasionally say things that are not true, but he will say them only because he knows his words will push you in the right direction.

I once heard a story that illustrates this. A rich man used to meditate once in a while. He had a Guru, an enlightened man, who used to tell him, 'You are not the mind or the body. You are the Self. Always abide as the Self.'

The man would listen attentively, but neither his meditation nor his Guru's words had much of an effect on him.

One day he approached his teacher and said, 'You have been telling me for years that I am not the mind and the body, and that I am the Self. I believe it and I meditate on this, but I don't see any changes in myself. This must be a very difficult technique because I don't seem to be making any progress with it.'

The Guru said, 'Let me look at your palm. I may be able to see something that is more suitable for you.'

After examining the disciple's palm, the Guru's face dropped.

'This is very bad. You should have put in more effort earlier in your life. I can see that you only have about one week to live. There's not much that can help you now.'

The disciple was shocked. He went home thinking, 'All my wealth and businesses are useless to me now. I put too much time into them, and not enough into my spiritual practice. There's nothing I can do now, but I can at least spend my last few days meditating.'

He went home and told his wife, 'My life is coming to an end. My Guru has warned me that this is my final week. I am going to spend my last few days meditating alone. Please tell my friends and relatives that I don't want to be disturbed.'

After a few days his Guru came to see how he was getting on.

'How's the meditation going?' he asked. 'Your wife tells me that you have done nothing else for days.'

'Gurudev, there is no one left to meditate. I have found the peace you have been talking about all these years.'

The Guru knew that this man would never focus full-time on realising the Self because he was too caught up with his family and his business affairs. By making him think that his death was imminent, he made him concentrate on what was real and important. And it worked.

This is not just a story; it is a tactic that will work for anyone. If you can withdraw energy from your worldly attachments and instead focus full-time on the Self, you will soon get results.

If you are having trouble with your enthusiasm for *sadhana*, just tell yourself, 'I may be dead in seven days'. Let go of all the things that you pretend are important in your daily life and instead focus on the Self for twenty-four hours a day. Do it and see what happens.

Question: It's not possible for some of us to make this kind of commitment. We have work to do, responsibilities in the world.

Annamalai Swami: *Sadhaks* should only work enough to maintain the body. Try to avoid unnecessary activities. Less work is good. Devote yourself to your *sadhana* all the time. You dissipate your desire for the Self by undertaking all kinds of useless activities that waste your time and lead to attachments. You think that your life is endless and that you can put off meditation till a later date. With this kind of attitude, you will die filled with regrets, not filled with peace.

If you have to engage in activity to support yourself or your family, then do it, but always be aware of the Self while you work. While you are doing that work keep your thoughts a hundred per cent on the Self.

You are what you think you are. You become what you think. If you think of the Self all the time, that is what you will become. If you live and die with thoughts of work and family, you will be reborn in a place with more work and more family business to worry about.

Question: What do you think of the common belief that a person's final thoughts determine his next birth?

Annamalai Swami: A rich man, who was very involved in his worldly affairs, was dying in his bed.

He called to his wife, 'Where is my oldest son?'

She replied, 'He is standing beside you, at the head of the bed.'

The wife was a meditative woman, and she also knew that her husband was about to die.

'Don't worry about worldly affairs at this time,' she advised. 'Relax peacefully into the Self. That's the most important thing at this time.'

The husband had other things on his mind. 'Where's my second son?' he asked.

'He is also beside the bed. Just try to keep quiet.'

'Then where is my youngest son?' demanded the man. 'I also need to know where he is.'

'He is here in the room with you. We are all here with you.'

'So who is looking after our shop if everyone is here?' asked the dying man, and a few seconds later he passed away.

This is how it is in life. If you spend your life with worldly thoughts, these will be the thoughts that fill your mind at the moment of your death. But if your life is devoted to *sadhana*, to attaining an inner peace, then, at the moment of your death, this will be the state that you die in.

18

Question: Is fasting beneficial? I have heard that thoughts diminish when one restricts one's food.

Annamalai Swami: This may happen, but one should be careful not to take it to extreme lengths. Bhagavan said that sattvic food in moderate quantities was the best external aid for *sadhaks*. Starving oneself will not produce long-term benefits. Bhagavan also advised that we should starve the mind of thoughts rather than starve the body of food. We need to keep the body in good health in order to do good *sadhana*. Depriving it of food and making it weak is not a step in the right direction.

One of Bhagavan's devotees, Lakshman Sharma, was a great advocate of naturopathy and fasting. He was a good devotee who wrote an excellent commentary on *Ulladu Narpadu*. Bhagavan gave him many lessons on this work, and Lakshman Sharma's commentary incorporated the explanations that Bhagavan himself gave.

During the 1940s a boy of about twenty years of age came from London. A bomb blast had affected his hearing. Lakshman Sharma wanted to treat him through naturopathy. Usually this involves going on a fast, although there are several other aspects to the treatment as well. The boy was put on a fast of several days, but unfortunately in this case there was no improvement. The fasting treatment was extended but the boy became weaker and weaker. Eventually, he became so weak, he died. Right until the end the boy was expecting that this treatment would cure him, but in the end it brought about his death.

These treatments have to be taken carefully. There are many people who will not be benefited by them.

Question: So we should make sure that we eat regularly?

Annamalai Swami: We should not force ourselves to eat if we are not hungry. Eat food when you feel hungry. Food always tastes better if you have an appetite for it. Eating food at times directed by others is far less satisfactory. If we take food at times when we have an appetite for it, we won't get sick. This is not just my advice. Avvayar, a great Tamil saint, gave this advice in one of her poems, and Tiruvalluvar, another of our great poet-saints, wrote, 'If you take your food only when you are hungry, you won't get sick. If you live like this, you will never have to go out in search of medicine.'

Question: I want to ask Swamiji a question. I want to relax more into the present and surrender to Bhagavan's will, but I am not sure that this is really within my power. In Swamiji's book, talk number five, Swamiji gave this answer: 'According to one's *prarabdha*, the efforts that are destined to happen will arise in one's mind.'

This is an extremely significant remark for me. As I understand it, all the activities that happen in this world happen according to Bhagavan's will. But the thoughts that instigate the actions also seem to come from Bhagavan, and are also predetermined.

Annamalai Swami: Yes, everything comes from Bhagavan. All our activities play themselves out as a manifestation of the divine will. Our karma is part of this destiny.

Question: OK. But I would still like to relax in the present and surrender to Bhagavan's will. I find that throughout the day thoughts are coming up. A thought comes up: 'I want to realise the Self.' I remind myself, 'Here and now I am the Self. This desire does not come from the Self, because the Self has no need of realising itself. So this must just be my *vasanas* coming up. I will ignore this thought.'

I cannot help this particular sequence of thoughts arising because Swami has said that these thoughts manifesting in that particular order is Bhagavan's will, my destiny. I might think that I am choosing a particular option or not, but that choice ultimately seems to be incorporated in my destiny. As I watch these thoughts arise, I feel that there is nothing I can do to end them, execute them, or indulge in them. I can surrender and watch them, but it doesn't seem that I can do anything more than that.

Annamalai Swami: Your thoughts arise on a moment-to-moment basis because of your *vasanas*, but it is a mistake to think that you can do nothing about them. You can be interested in them, or you can ignore them. If you show interest in them, they will persist and you will get caught up in them. If you ignore them and keep your attention on the source, they will not develop. And when they don't develop, they disappear.

In *Who Am I?* Bhagavan compared this process to laying siege to a fort. If you cut off, one by one, the heads of the thoughts as they come out of the fort of the mind, sooner or later there will be none left. The way to do this is by self-enquiry. As each thought rises, you ask yourself, 'To whom does this thought appear?' If you are vigilant in doing this, the forest of thoughts will lessen and lessen until there are none left. When the thoughts have gone, mind will sink into its source and experience that source.

Question: I want to understand this process of ignoring thoughts. Thoughts will arise: 'I want to realise the Self'; 'I have not realised the Self'; or, 'I must do such-and-such a practice to realise the Self'. I realise that these are all desires, all *vasanas*, so I say to myself, 'I am the Self. Here and now I am the Self.' As Swamiji says, this seems to stop the flow of thoughts for a while. I try to hold onto the 'I'-thought, as Swamiji recommends, but I don't seem to have any real control over it. I still feel that whether I succeed or not is Bhagavan's will, something that is not within my control. I feel helpless. I remember that whenever the mind moves, it is on a wild goose chase, that it is chasing phantoms that don't exist. So I remember Swamiji's advice and remind myself, 'I am the Self here and now'. It helps, but not for long. Thoughts still come up again.

Annamalai Swami: Suppose you are walking down a busy road. You encounter all kinds of people doing all kinds of things. Little conversations are going on in one place. Perhaps workmen are digging a hole somewhere. Inside a store a customer may be arguing about the price of some goods, while in the middle of the road there may be a crowd of people congregating around an accident victim. None of this is your business, but there is always a possibility that you will get interested in some or all of these activities and forget the reason why you are out on the street yourself. Don't get excited by anything you see and hear. Just walk steadily towards your destination.

Your *vasanas* are all the sideshows in your head that can drag your attention away from your main business, which is being aware of the Self. If you have no interest in them, you will walk straight to your goal. If something temporarily distracts your attention, bring yourself back by asking yourself, 'Who is interested in all this? Who is getting interested in this distraction?' This will deflate the distracting desire and it will bring you back to an awareness of your true purpose.

Remember, nothing that happens in the mind is 'you', and none of it is your business.

You don't have to worry about thoughts that rise up inside you.

It is enough that you remember that the thoughts are not you.

Question: That goes for all kinds of thoughts?

Annamalai Swami: Whatever kind of thought arises, have the same reaction: 'Not me; not my business.' It can be a good thought or a bad thought. Treat them all the same way. To whom are these thoughts arising? To you. That means that you are not the thought.

You are the Self. Remain as the Self, and don't latch onto anything that is not the Self.

Question: There is another thing that comes up for me: there is a desire for the earnestness to remember the Self all the time. The mind will latch onto this and think, 'I should meditate more. I should pay more attention to being in the present.' Ideas such as these set off whole chains of thought. Yet this still looks to me to be an effort by the ego to realise the Self that is already here. In some ways it seems to me to be another distraction.

Annamalai Swami: If you remain as the Self, no *vasanas* and no karma will touch or affect you. If you remain in the mind, thoughts of one sort or another will bother you all the time.

Question: If I understand correctly, my karma is all the activities that my body has to undertake in this life. I can be a witness to it but I cannot change it. If I pick up this glass that is in front of me, it happened because it was my karma to pick it up in this moment. I don't have a choice. Either I am destined to pick it up, or I am not. Bhagavan said the same thing. When someone picked up a fan and asked if that act was destined from the moment he was born, Bhagavan said, 'Yes, it was destined'.

Annamalai Swami: If the thoughts 'I should meditate' or 'I should realise' arise, ask yourself, 'To whom are these thoughts arising?' Why do you need to think about your body and your mind so much? If you are the light, there is no darkness. If you are the Self, there is no thought, no body, and no mind to give you any trouble. Any number of thoughts may come. Let them. But remember all the time, 'I am the Self'. You are not the *vasanas*, you are not the thoughts, you are the Self. Keep that awareness and don't worry too much about what is going on in your mind, and what it means.

Don't allow any identifications to settle on you. Don't think, 'I am sitting in Bhagavan's shrine.' Don't think, 'I am doing, I am acting, I am sitting'.

You are the Self, not the body. Even your *vasanas* are the Self. All is your Self. There are no distinctions, no differences in the Self. Nothing is separate from the Self. You cannot find a single atom, a single thought that is apart from the Self. All is the Self.

Question: But is there anything I can do to discover this? Is not all effort pointless if everything that happens to me is predetermined?

Annamalai Swami: All these doubts that are troubling you arise simply because you are enmeshed in the 'I am the body' thought and all the confusing consequences that it brings. It is more productive to keep the awareness 'I am the Self' than to be analysing the usefulness of effort. *Sadhana*, effort and practice, and any ideas you may have about them, are concepts that can only arise when you believe that you are not the Self, and when you believe that you have to do something to reach the Self.

Even the sequence, 'To whom has this thought come? To me,' is based on ignorance of the truth. Why? Because it is verbalising a state of ignorance; it is perpetuating an erroneous assumption that there is a person who is having troublesome thoughts. You are the Self, not some make-believe person who is having thoughts.

If you remain in the Self, as the Self, no harm can come to you. In that state, whatever comes to you will not be a problem. There is no duality when you remain as the Self; no thoughts about what you should or should not do, and no thoughts about what can be done or what can't be done. The main thing is not to go out of the Self. When you have switched on the light, darkness cannot come, not even if you desire it.

Question: Swamiji frequently says that we should meditate constantly to stay in the Self. I find that I cannot meditate constantly. When I realise that I am not meditating, the mind tells me that I should do something to get back into the Self. This is my real state, my actual condition. I cannot stay constantly in the Self.

Annamalai Swami: When this thought, 'I am not meditating,' or 'I am not in the Self,' arises, just ignore it and go back to the Self. When thoughts such as these arise, look at them and think, 'Not me, not my business,' and go back to the Self. Don't waste energy on thinking or evaluating how well or how badly you are doing in your meditation.

Question: When attentiveness has been lost, when I realise that I am not in the present, that I am not meditating, the mind is inevitably distracted. The thought, the evaluation, always comes: 'I am distracted.'

Annamalai Swami: Whatever thoughts come, ignore them. You have to ignore anything that is connected to the body-mind idea, anything that is based on the notion that you are the mind or the body. If you can do this, the rising thought will not disturb or distract you. In a split second, it will run away.

All thoughts are distractions, including the thought 'I am meditating'. If you are the Self, darkness will not overcome you. Whatever thoughts arise in that state won't affect you.

Question: Is the ability to remember 'I am the Self' part of one's destiny?

Annamalai Swami: If you are the Self, no destiny will affect you. If you tear your shirt, does that mean that you are also torn? No. Something has happened to something that is not you. Similarly, the body and the mind will experience pleasure, happiness, misery, and so on, all according to the karma that has been brought into this life. But the Self has no attachment, no detachment, no happiness, no unhappiness and no karma. The body is not the Self; the mind is not the Self. The real 'I' is the Self, and nothing ever happens to or affects the Self.

Thoughts will come as long as the potential for them is inside you. Good thoughts, bad thoughts, they will all keep coming. There is nothing you can do about this flow, but at the same time, this flow of thoughts need not be a problem. Be the Self, be the peace that is your real nature, and it will not matter what comes up. Walk, eat, drink, sleep, meditate, but never think that you are the one who is doing these things. The thought that you are doing something is the thought that is poisoning your life. Because once you think that you are doing something, you will start to think that you need to be doing something else to put yourself in a better situation. You don't have to do anything to experience the nectar of the Self. All you need to do is drop the idea that you are doing anything at all.

You need to change your vision, your perspective. When you live in the mind and see a world outside you that is separate and apart from you, you will make plans, you will worry, you will have doubts such as the ones you have been telling me about today. These doubts keep coming up in you because you are not dwelling in the source, the substratum. In that place there is oneness, a oneness in which all distinctions, all separation is absent.

If you abide as the Self, you will see the world as the Self. In fact, there will be no world at all. No world, no *maya*, no mind, no distinctions of any kind. It is like the state of seeing only wood in the carved elephant, only threads in the dyed cloth. In that state of being and knowing the Self, ideas of right and wrong, things to do and things to avoid doing, will vanish. You will know that they were just mental concepts. In that state you will know that mind is the Self, bondage is the Self, everything is the Self. With that vision, nothing will bind you; nothing will cause you misery.

The Self may appear as the manifest world, as different separate objects, but the underlying reality, the only real substance is the Self in which they are all appearing and disappearing. Things and people may appear in this substratum, and you may use them or interact with them, but your peace will never be disturbed.

When you abide as the Self, there is no one left to choose and decide. Life goes on automatically. You will pick up the things that are needed, and not pick up the things that are not needed. What you pick up and what you don't pick up will not be a consequence of what you like or dislike. These preferences will not be there any more.

This perspective will be yours when you give up or cease to believe the idea, 'I am different from the world'. Giving up this thought is a great *sadhana* in itself. Abandoning this false idea will be enough to give you peace.

When the thought is there, the world seems to be full of good people and bad people, all busily engaged in doing what appear to you to be good things and bad things. When the thought is absent, you know them all to be your own Self. In that state you won't like them, dislike them or judge them, or be aware of them as being other than your own Self. This absence of likes, dislikes and judgements will leave you in your original natural state of peace.

Teeth and tongue are both parts of you, and they both function in harmony, without fighting or struggling. When there is the knowledge that mind and Self are one, there will be no fights, no struggles, and no attempts to judge or attain. To have this harmony, place the mind in the Self and keep it there. This is the real meditation. However, until you reach this state in which there are no distinctions and preferences, you should use a little discrimination with regard to who and what you associate with. Avoid bad company and bad thoughts, and try to keep the conviction that nothing is separate from you.

During sleep you have no likes and dislikes. *Jnanis* and babies manage this while they are awake. Baby mind is good; *jnani* mind is good; 'I am the body' mind is very, very bad.

Question: It's a poisonous thought!

Annamalai Swami: Yes, yes. The 'I am the body' thought is just as poisonous as a cobra.

'All is my Self. All is the nectar of my own Self.' These are the great affirmations that counter the 'I am the body' thought. Holding on to one of these sayings is the equal of millions of *punyas*. If we continuously meditate on the truth of these statements, if we hold on to the truth that they are pointing towards, countless *punyas* will accrue to us.

There are many other mantras, but none are as useful as these. *Ribhu Gita* says, 'All is one. All is the Self.' This is the truth that you have to hold onto. To the real 'I', nothing is foreign in the entire universe. If you know you are everything, there will be no desire to pursue some things and not others. Nothing will be liked more or less than anything else. Do you like or desire your arm more than your foot? When your body is the whole universe, likes, dislikes and desires will be absent.

Question: I know that the *jnani* has no dislikes and no preferences, but I have to admit I am different. I have a strong desire to be in your presence. I believe that being here is doing me good, so I stay. [Addressing the translator] Here I have a beautiful feeling that no one has loved me as he does.

Annamalai Swami: Drop the body-mind idea and you will discover that you don't have any likes or dislikes. You do not think that your shirt is yourself. Similarly, the *jnani* does not believe that he is his body or his mind. The *jnani* understands that the body and the mind are animated by the Self, but he also knows that he shines as the Self whether the body and mind are there or not.

Without the Self, the body and the mind can do nothing at all. You could not eat, sleep, speak, or do anything at all without the Self.

Keep your body in good condition if you want to, but don't ever believe that it is you. You can keep your car in good working order without ever believing that you are the car. Have the same attitude towards your body. You are not your car and you are not your body. Both will perish, but the Self will continue because it is always there. When you identify with transient things that pass away or perish, you too will pass away and perish, but when you identify with the Self, you will not pass away or change in any way. The Self has no birth, no death, no bondage, no misery, no youth, no old age, and no sickness. These are attributes of changing bodies and minds, not the Self. Be the Self and none of these things will ever happen to you.

19

Question: Ramana Maharshi told you to leave his ashram because, you say, he wanted you not to be attached to his form. You had already contacted the formless, and you knew that the Maharshi was not the form you saw in the ashram.

It seems to me that the physical form is not that important. It seems to me that it is more important to find God, the Self, in the Heart. This leads me to the question of how important it is to have a physical Master. In order to realise the Self, do we need to have a physical Master? For myself, I am beginning to feel more and more that it has nothing to do with a physical form, but sometimes I have doubts. Am I just fooling myself by believing that I can contact the Self within without the aid of an external physical Master?

Annamalai Swami: If you go to a physical Guru and ask him how to realise the Self, he will probably tell you that you are already the Self, and that you should just hold onto the Self that you already are. If you can manage that you will be with the true Guru all the time, and you will not need the physical form of the Guru to keep reminding you of who you are. In that state you will be living with Bhagavan, staying as the Self, holding onto the real 'I' at all times.

If you go to the physical form of the Guru and ask about Self-realisation, you will not be told about the importance of the physical form of the Guru. You will be told to hold onto the real 'I'. You will be told that you should not fall into the trap of believing that the Guru is just a body. The Guru is inside you as the Self and outside you as a physical form that has manifested in the Self. If you follow the advice that the physical Guru gives, you will discover that the inner and outer Gurus are one and the same.

However, very few people can manage this by themselves.

Question: Is there still work to be done after the Self is reached and experienced?

Annamalai Swami: Initially, abidance in the Self may not be firm and irreversible. Vigilance may be needed at first to maintain it.

There is a verse from *Kaivalya Navaneeta* that Bhagavan often quoted. It speaks of the need for vigilance even after the Self has been experienced for the first time. In the verse the disciple is speaking to his Guru:

'Lord, you are the reality remaining as my inmost Self, ruling me during all my countless incarnations! Glory to you who have put on an external form in order to instruct me. I do not see how I can repay your grace for having liberated me. Glory! Glory to your holy feet!'

The Guru replies:

'To stay fixed in the Self without the three kinds of obstacles [ignorance, uncertainty and wrong knowledge] obstructing your experience, is the highest return you can render me.'

The Guru knows that without vigilance, an initial experience of the Self may slip away.

Question: Why is this initial experience not enough?

Annamalai Swami: If *vasanas* are still there, they will rise up again and the experience will be lost. While they are there, there is always the possibility that we may again take the unreal to be real.

If we take the mirage to be real water, that is ignorance. Similarly, if we take the unreal body to be the Self, that is also ignorance. As soon as ignorance comes, you must question it. 'To whom does this ignorance come?' A strong determination to pursue enquiry in this way will dissolve all doubts. By questioning 'Who am I?' and by constantly meditating, one comes to the clarity of being.

As long as *vasanas* continue to exist they will rise and cover the reality, obscuring awareness of it. As often as you become aware of them, question, 'To whom do they come?' This continuous enquiry will establish you in your own Self and you will have no further problems. When you know that the snake of the mind never existed, when you know that the rope of reality is all that exists, doubts and fears will not trouble you again.

Question: What is it that brings maturity and growth in a person? How do the *gunas* change in such a way that the mind eventually becomes sattvic?

Annamalai Swami: Self has no birth, no death, no sufferings and no problems. It is the witness of all these phenomena, but it is untouched by them. All these experiences happen to the mind, and through numerous lives the mind lives, learns and matures. It takes a body and learns some lessons in that body. Then it takes another form, another body and learns something else. The mind goes on like this for innumerable lifetimes until finally it has learned enough to go back to its source, the Self.

Question: Do the five sheaths, the *kosas*, mature in this process? Do some of them mature, or do all of them?

Annamalai Swami: Mind includes all the five *kosas*. Through many lifetimes one can say that the *kosas* are maturing and growing, but realisation ultimately has nothing to do with a mature mind or mature *kosas*. It is the state in which one transcends the five *kosas* and the mind. It is the state in which one finally understands that the mind, whether mature or immature, never really existed.

Question: Does the acquisition of spiritual knowledge make the mind mature?

Annamalai Swami: The acquisition of knowledge belongs to the realm of education, not *sadhana*. Seeing everything as one is the true seeing, and controlling the five senses in the body is the true *sadhana*. They must be controlled, and success in this endeavour is truly heroic. No traditional education can prepare you for this. Realising the Self is the true education.

One of Mahatma Gandhi's disciples was educated to a very high level. He was also a pious man and a strict disciplinarian with himself. When he realised that all he wanted in life was Self-realisation, he tore up all his academic certificates and threw them away. He knew that neither his education nor his worldly knowledge would help him. In fact by doing this he implied that his knowledge was a hindrance that had to be rejected.

A proper education does not come from books. It comes from associating with *jnanis*. They alone can guide us and teach us properly. I served Bhagavan for twelve years. Looking back on those years I can now say that just as you cannot get a proper formal academic education without attending school, one cannot get a true spiritual education without *satsang*, either with a *jnani* or with one's own Self.

20

Question: It is difficult for me to stay focussed on the 'I'-thought, especially when I am in the middle of worldly activities. Is it enough to be aware of awareness, of consciousness in general?

Annamalai Swami: If you are conscious of consciousness, there is no duality. Everything is included in consciousness.

Question: But is it enough to be aware of the awareness?

Annamalai Swami: You are repeating the question, so I will repeat the answer. If you remain in the state of consciousness, there will be nothing apart from it. No problems, no misery, no questions.

Question: Are you always in that state of consciousness? I find that when I am busy with activities, thoughts come up and I am no longer remembering myself. I am no longer focussing on consciousness.

Annamalai Swami: I don't lose consciousness of the Self because I don't get identified with the body and the mind. It is only in the state in which you identify with the body and the mind that problems arise.

In deep sleep we forget the body and the mind, but consciousness is still there. That same state is present now, while we are awake. If you give up all your ideas about separateness, that will be enough. When those ideas have gone you realise you are everything.

Question: In the *Ribhu Gita* it is mentioned that bad qualities and good qualities are both *Brahman*. Does that mean that we don't need to care about good and bad qualities?

Annamalai Swami: In your real state there is only consciousness. In deep sleep no names and forms manifest in that consciousness, whereas in the dreaming and waking state they do. When you look at a piece of cloth, you notice its name-and-form attributes: the colour, the design, the thickness, etc. But what you are really looking at is just threads. The underlying nature of consciousness, the equivalent of the threads in the cloth, is peace. To abide knowingly as consciousness is to be a deep, undisturbed peace, even though thoughts and activities may be manifesting in it. When you see through the eyes of wisdom, there is only peace. No bondage or *samsara* touches you. Even to say that the Self is peace is not quite correct. I call it peace, but really, it is not something that can be described or defined by words.

Good and bad qualities are ideas that manifest in the mind, in *samsara*. They are concepts that vanish when only this peace remains. When you are peace, when you are consciousness, all good qualities will manifest in you and through 'you, but you will not be aware of them as being 'good'. You will just be that peace.

Question: The wheel of life – manifestation, *samsara* – seems to continue whether one is established in that peace or not. Is there nothing in this manifestation that provides a key to peace?

Annamalai Swami: If you understand the true nature of this wheel of life, this wheel that is giving everyone so much alternating happiness and misery, this understanding will lead you to where there is no wheel, no change, no movement. This wheel is spinning in the substratum of the changeless Self. If you take your position in the still, peaceful centre of the Self you will know, simultaneously, that the Self is motionless peace, and that the spinning wheel is also the Self.

Question: Why is there a need to have this spinning wheel in the Self? Why a need for manifestation at all?

Annamalai Swami: This question is happening only in your mind. If you remain in the Self, as the Self, the question will not arise. Whether you move your hand or keep it still, it is still a hand. Its nature is not changed in either case. *Maya* is the Self. All is the Self. If you give up all distinctions, you will know this for yourself. That's all you need to do.

Question: Why does the mind always go outwards instead of inwards?

Annamalai Swami: Because we don't ask the question, 'Why does the mind go outwards instead of inwards?'

This question arises because the nature of happiness is not properly understood. People are always looking for it in the wrong places and by doing the wrong activities. You begin with the impression, which is really a misunderstanding, that happiness is something that can be found outside you, and furthermore, that you have to do something or go somewhere to reach it. This is your illusion, and it is your belief in this illusion that makes the mind search for happiness in the outside world.

Even when you are told, 'Happiness is within you as your own Self. Look inwards and find it,' still you think that you have to do something or go somewhere to discover it. This is the power of *maya*, of illusion. This is like one fish in the sea asking another fish for directions to the ocean.

When you are not aware that your glasses are resting on your nose, you may look for them all day, thinking that they are lost. As a consequence, you believe that they are an object to be found. Eventually, you realise that you were wearing them all the time.

While the search was on, that which was being sought was, in reality, that through which the seeing was taking place. You were looking for an object that finally turned out to be the subject that was doing the seeing. So it is with the mind and the Self. Mind sets up the notion that the Self needs to be found, and then proceeds to hunt for it as if it were some object that could be located in some interior place. This is as foolish as a man with a goat wrapped round his shoulders spending his time wandering around, looking for his goat, and asking everyone he meets where it might be.

Question: You say that I am the Self, and that I don't even need to look inwards to discover it. I think that grace is needed to experience the truth of this statement since effort of any kind seems to be counterproductive.

Annamalai Swami: Grace is always present, always available, but for it to be effective, one must be in a state to receive it and make full use of it. If you want to take a full cup of water from a lake, you have fully to immerse the cup first. If you want to fill your mind with grace, submerge it fully in the Self. In that place the grace will manifest in you as peace and happiness.

Question: Does the mind die gradually or suddenly?

Annamalai Swami: One answer is: 'When the sun comes up, does darkness disappear suddenly or gradually?'

Bhagavan, speaking on this topic, once remarked: 'Someone mistakes a rope hanging in the darkness for a snake. He then asks how many years it will take for the snake to die.'

This is a better answer. If the mind does not exist, it cannot die either quickly or slowly.

Glossary

advaita	Non-duality; the Hindu philosophical school that expounds this teaching.
ananda	Bliss.
Brahman	The impersonal ultimate reality of Hinduism.
darshan	Seeing or being seen by a holy person or temple deity.
giri pradakshina	Walking around a mountain; in this book it always means circumambulating Arunachala.
gunas	See *rajas*.
jnana	Transcendental knowledge; true knowing.
jnani	One who has attained *jnana*.
karmas	Actions; the activities or work that one is destined to do in this life.
kaupina	A loincloth made of two pieces of cloth, one tied around the waist and the other between the legs.
kosas	In yogic philosophy there are five *kosas* or sheaths through which the *jiva*, the individual self, functions.
lingam	A vertical column of stone with a rounded upper end that is worshipped as a repesentation or embodiment of Siva.

mahasamadhi	The moment when an enlightened being gives up his body and physically dies.
maya	Illusion; the power that makes the unreal world seem to be real.
moksha	Spiritual liberation.
papam	See *punya*.
prarabdha	The destined acts that the body has to perform in this life.
puja	Ritual worship of a Hindu deity.
Purnavasu	One of the twenty-seven 'star days' in the Hindu calendar. These star days are used to calculate the timing of birthdays and other annually celebrated events.
punya	Meritoroius acts or the consequences of them. Most Hindus believe that one's actions produce an accumulation of karma that has to be experienced at a future date. An accumulation of *punyas*, or good actions, will result in an auspicious rebirth in which one will reap the beneficial consequences of one's earlier good behaviour, whereas an accumumulation of *papams*, sinful, evil or bad acts) will result in the opposite.
rajas	One of the three *gunas*, or qualities of being, that make up all manifestation, including the mind. *Rajas* manifests as agitation, activity, passion; *tamas* as inertia, darkness, ignorance; *sattva* as harmony, purity, brightness.

Sadguru	A fully enlightened Guru who is established in *sat*, beingness.
sadhak	One whose life is dedicated to performing *sadhana*.
samadhi	A deep meditative state in which one has a direct awareness of the Self, without having any consciousness of the body; the grave of a Hindu saint or enlightened being.
samsara	The cycle of birth and death; manifestation of the world; the mechanism by which unfulfilled desires create new births and new worlds in which these desires can be fulfilled.
satsang	Literally 'association with truth'; being in the company of an enlightened being; association with those who are seeking enlightenment; maintaining awareness of the Self within.
tamas	See *rajas*.
tapas	Spiritual practice in which there is some element of self-denial or bodily mortification.
vasanas	The tendencies of the mind; the conditioned responses of the the mind; the energy inherent in thoughts that makes them rise and demand attention or action.
vibhuti	Sacred ash, usually distributed at the end of Hindu rituals.